The Bedford/St. Martin's ESL Workbook

The Bedford/St. Martin's ESL Workbook

Second Edition

Sapna Gandhi-Rao
University of Louisville

Maria McCormack
Columbia University

Elizabeth Trelenberg
Florida State University

Bedford/St. Martin's

Boston ■ New York

Manufactured in the United States of America.

8 7 6 5 4
i h g f e

For information, write: Bedford/St. Martin's, 75 Arlington Street, Boston, MA 02116   (617-399-4000)

ISBN-10: 0-312-54034-5
ISBN-13: 978-0-312-54034-0

Contents

To the Instructor

The discussions and exercises in this workbook are designed to provide additional instruction and practice for students who are non-native speakers of English. The 112 exercise sets cover the grammar, punctuation, mechanics, and usage issues that ESL students typically find challenging.

Most of the exercise sets are written as connected discourse with a thematic focus that allows students to read and revise their work in context. You may wish to assign some of these exercises in conjunction with topics covered in class, or you may prefer to have students work on specific difficulties you've identified in their writing. The answers to all exercises are provided in an appendix so that students may check their work independently.

The last exercise in each section is a writing prompt that encourages students to write their own paragraph, applying the grammar covered in that section. These prompts, called "Taking the Next Step," can be assigned as soon as students complete the exercises in each section, while the material studied is still fresh. The workbook's editing guidelines and glossary help students understand editing conventions and unfamiliar terms.

More exercises are available on Exercise Central, the online exercise database at bedfordstmartins.com/exercisecentral, and on the CD-ROM, *Exercise Central to Go: Writing and Grammar Practice for Basic Writers*.

If you would like more information about these materials or about the complete supplements package for your textbook, please contact your local Bedford/St. Martin's sales representative or e-mail sales_support@bfwpub.com.

Acknowledgments

We wish to thank the following reviewers who graciously provided feedback and suggestions. Mary T. Bailey, Palm Beach Community College; Anne Lambert, Guilford Technical Community College; Carol A. Munroe, College of the Desert; Linda Muñoz, Texas State University–San Marcos; Connie Ross, Ocean County College; Mary Ann Simoneau, California State University–Stanislaus.

To the Student

The difference between the formal English you use in your writing and the informal English you use in everyday conversation complicates the already formidable task of learning the English language. In fact, formal English can sometimes seem like a completely different language from conversational English. But just as practice in listening to and speaking English helps your conversational skills, practice in reading and writing English will help your writing skills.

This book was designed to help you master formal written English by providing extensive grammar practice through exercises. The book is organized into parts based on particular grammar areas; the exercises range from basic identification tasks to fill-in-the-blank activities to locating grammatical errors within texts. At the end of each section you will find an exercise entitled "Taking the Next Step." These exercises are intended to keep you thinking about the skills you've practiced and to help you put them to use in your own writing.

Whether you use this book in conjunction with other writing textbooks or use it alone to hone your writing skills, we hope that you become more confident writing in English as you strengthen your abilities.

Part 1
Nouns

A noun is a word that names a person (*sister, fireman*), place (*mountains, supermarket*), thing (*chair, peanut butter*), or concept (*love, pain*). Proper nouns name specific people, places, things, or concepts (*Maria, Nevada, Ford Theater, Confucianism*). Collective nouns name groups (*dozen, gang*). Nouns that have both singular and plural forms are called **count nouns**.

Singular and Plural Nouns

Nouns that end in **consonant + *y*** form the plural by replacing the **-*y*** with **-*i*** and adding **-*es***.

Singular	Plural
party	parties
baby	babies
lady	ladies

Some nouns do not follow these rules in forming the plural. It is helpful to memorize these irregular plural forms as you encounter them.

Singular	Plural	Singular	Plural
man	men	woman	women
child	children	ox	oxen
foot	feet	goose	geese
mouse	mice	sheep	sheep
fish	fish	stimulus	stimuli

Note that patterns in forming the plural exist even within these irregular plural forms.

Count Nouns

Count nouns are used for items that you can count individually. Most count nouns add **-*s*** or **-*es*** to form the plural.

-*s*		-*es*	
book	books	watch	watches
car	cars	kiss	kisses
ocean	oceans	dress	dresses
desk	desks	potato	potatoes
ant	ants	tomato	tomatoes
hand	hands	bus	buses

Noncount Nouns

Noncount nouns are used for items that do not have a plural form and cannot be counted unless you add a quantity (*carton of* <u>milk</u>, *head of* <u>lettuce</u>, *gallons of* <u>gasoline</u>).

Food and drink

bread	cocoa	milk
butter	coffee	pasta
cabbage	corn	rice
candy	flour	salt
cereal	fruit	sugar
cheese	ice	tea
chicken	meat	water

Gases, liquids, and materials

air	gold	plastic
alcohol	helium	rain
blood	iron	steel
gasoline	oxygen	wood

Abstract nouns

advice	happiness	love
anger	health	poverty
beauty	information	truth
courage	knowledge	wealth
freedom		

Other common noncount nouns

clothing	money	weather
furniture	research	work
grass	traffic	

Some nouns can be either count or noncount, depending on their meaning in the sentence.

Count   **Grains**, such as rice, should be eaten every day for a healthy diet.

Noncount Horses and chickens consume a great amount of **grain** every day.

When learning new nouns in English, you should consult a dictionary or a reliable online source to determine whether a noun is count, noncount, or both.

Exercise 1.1 Singular and Plural Nouns

For each of the following sentences, underline the appropriate singular or plural noun from the pair in parentheses.

Example: Immigration in the early twentieth century was a very important (<u>period</u>/periods) in U.S. history.

1. Many (immigrant/immigrants) to the United States at the turn of the twentieth century came from Europe.

2. They crossed hundreds of miles of (ocean/oceans) to escape poverty and political problems.

3. Many immigrants were fleeing from disease, which killed thousands of Europeans in many (country/countries).

4. Immigrants also came from different (corner/corners) of the world to the United States to seek new opportunities.

5. Problems drove some people away from their native countries, but others came to the United States because they wanted to own a few acres of (land/lands) or find opportunities that were unavailable at home.

6. One of the most important (port/ports) of entry for immigrants to the United States was Ellis Island in New York Harbor.

7. When they arrived at Ellis Island, immigrants had to pass a number of (test/tests).

8. Anyone with symptoms of tuberculosis, smallpox, or other contagious (disease/diseases) had to return home on a departing ship.

9. Some immigrants spoke little English, and people from certain cultures were also unfamiliar with the twenty-six (letter/letters) of the alphabet used in the United States.

10. Many immigration (official/officials) at Ellis Island gave these people Americanized names.

Exercise 1.2 Singular and Plural Nouns

Revise each sentence to correct any errors in the use of singular and plural noun forms. Some sentences might not contain any errors.

Example: The Beatles broke up more than thirty year ago.

1. The Beatles were one of the most popular musical act of all time.

2. Four young man from Liverpool, England, made a fortune playing songs that young people loved.

3. Recordings by the Beatles still sell millions of copy today.

4. Some buyers are middle-aged fans who have not lost respects for the group.

5. They may buy CDs since they no longer own stereo equipment that can play their old vinyl records.

6. Playing musics from their youth makes some fans feel young again.

7. Other people who buy Beatles records are teenager discovering the songs for the first time.

8. Even today, a teenager is likely to know bits of Beatle trivias.

9. Some young listeners become fans, but others don't understand the fusses about the Beatles.

10. The two surviving Beatles are in their mid-sixties, but their fans span all age.

Exercise 1.3 Singular and Plural Nouns

Using the word in parentheses, fill in the blank with the appropriate singular or plural form.

Example: The pony express ended when the _____*telegraph*_____ (telegraph) crossed the United States.

1. The United States Postal Service is the oldest _____ (agency) of the federal government.

2. It was formally established in 1775 after several _____ (attempt) by private citizens, the British government, and local statesmen to create a system for sending and receiving mail.

3. Benjamin Franklin played an important _____ (role) in making the service efficient, safe, and profitable.

4. Mail was delivered by horseback, and riders carried _____ (mail) from Maine to Florida.

5. Every 75 miles, each rider would hand over the mail _____ (pack) to the next rider.

6. Riders were very careful to protect the mail, so the colonists could feel that their written _____ (communication) was safe.

7. One famous U.S. _____ (president), Abraham Lincoln, also served as postmaster.

8. The Postal Service is part of the federal government and as the _____ (country) grew, so did the power of the Postal Service.

9. Horseback wasn't the only method for delivering the mail; it was also delivered by steamboat and by _____ (train).

10. Since its establishment, the Postal Service has served the American people in _____ (time) of peace and war.

Exercise 1.4 Count and Noncount Nouns

Underline the appropriate noun in each of the following sentences.

> **Example:** Early immigrants to the United States often got bad (<u>information</u>/informations) about their new country.

1. A large (number/amount) of European immigrants moved to the United States by steamboat.

2. The new immigrants had different (reason/reasons) for leaving their homeland to come to this country.

3. Many immigrants came here seeking new opportunities for (freedom/freedoms).

4. Also, many (family/families) wished to be reunited with their loved ones.

5. (Overpopulation/Overpopulations), famine, and disease also drove people to leave their homeland.

6. In addition, (discrimination/discriminations) by the government and police in some countries spurred emigration.

7. Immigrants to the United States have often faced (battle/battles) with current residents over jobs, housing, and their facility with English.

8. (Legislation/Legislations) to discourage immigration increased in the last decade of the twentieth century.

9. For example, the Immigration Reform Act of 1995 made it clear that immigrants have to become citizens before they can qualify for Social Security (benefit/benefits).

10. Many immigrants today need the (advice/advices) of other immigrants, government officials, and social service agencies to learn what rights they have.

Exercise 1.5 Count and Noncount Nouns

Underline the appropriate noun from the pair in parentheses.

Example: Most people look forward to taking long (vacation/<u>vacations</u>).

Hawaii is a chain of (1.) (island/islands) in the Pacific Ocean. The warm (2.) (weather/weathers) brings visitors from all over the world. The abundance of (3.) (fruit/fruits) is also an attraction; there's nothing like eating a fresh (4.) (pineapple/pineapples) for breakfast. Another attraction is the natural beauty of Hawaii's geographical (5.) (feature/features) such as volcanoes, waterfalls, and beaches. Enjoying the natural beauty is a great way to find (6.) (relief/reliefs) from a hectic lifestyle. Hawaii also has many natural (7.) (resource/resources). One of them is (8.) (coffee/coffees). Visitors will also find many spas promoting (9.) (relaxation/relaxations). Certainly, Hawaii has inspired many (10.) (people/peoples) to visit again.

Exercise 1.6 Taking the Next Step with Nouns

Write about your favorite foods and any new foods you've tried recently. What are the ingredients? How are these foods cooked? Where did you eat these foods (at home, at a friend's house, in a restaurant)? Be sure to use singular and plural nouns, count and noncount nouns, and the new vocabulary you learned in this chapter. Refer to the relevant sections of this chapter as you work to help master each concept.

_____

_____

_____

_____

_____

_____

_____

_____

_____

Part 2
Articles

The articles *a/an* and *the* belong to a class of modifiers called **determiners**. This workbook treats articles separately from other determiners because they can pose particular difficulties for non-native speakers of English.

A/An

A/an are called **indefinite articles** and are used to modify nonspecific count nouns (*an apple, a car*). Nonspecific nouns give general information only. *An* is a variant of *a* that occurs directly before a word beginning with a vowel sound (not simply beginning with a vowel—pay attention to the way the word *sounds* rather than how it is *spelled*).

 a university **an** umbrella
 a towel   **an** hour

A/an may precede a noun, adjective, or adverb, but it must modify a noun.

 a big blue umbrella
 an unusually big umbrella

You should use the indefinite article *a/an* when the reader is not likely to know the identity of the noun being modified. Use *a/an* when introducing a noun for the first time.

 On the first day of class, **a** woman came in and announced that the class would move to another room.

In this sentence, *a* modifies the noun *woman* because the reader doesn't know who the woman is.

The

The is a **definite article** because it is only used for specific people, places, things, and ideas (*the President of the United States, the* Titanic). *The* should also be used with the superlative and with ordinal numerals (*the first, the sixth*).

 On the first day of class, a woman came in and announced that the class would move to another room. **The** woman led all the students down the hallway.

The modifies *woman* in the second sentence above since the writer is referring to the woman whom we now know.

 A boy stepped out of his house and began calling his dog. **The** dog came running down **the** street.

The reader doesn't know the identity of the boy, so the indefinite article *a* is used in the first sentence. Because the first sentence specifies the identity of the dog—*his* dog—the definite article *the* is appropriate in the second sentence. The reader assumes the street is the one in front of the boy's house, so again the definite article *the* is appropriate.

Put **the** milk in **the** refrigerator.

In the example above, the reader can assume that there is only one container of milk and only one refrigerator.

This is **the** best pie I've ever eaten.

The superlative *best* identifies the noun *pie*.

Zero Article

The term *zero article* indicates that there is no need for an article. Zero article occurs only with noncount or plural count forms, and it signifies general categories.

I'm afraid to ride **roller coasters**.

She likes **flowers**. **Roses** are her favorite flower.

Our dog liked to chase **cats**.

Note that you do not use *a/an* and *the* with other determiners such as *his*, *its*, *those*, and so on.

Exercise 2.1 Articles

For each of the following sentences, underline the appropriate article from the words in parentheses. **X** means "no article."

> **Example:** (A/An/<u>The</u>/X) love of two people can transcend cultural differences.

1. (A/An/The/X) marriage that unites people from different cultures can be very difficult.

2. There are many obstacles to overcome if they wish for (a/an/the/X) marriage to be successful.

3. One might consider learning about (a/an/the/X) cultural expectations before entering into such a permanent contract.

4. In some countries, people believe that men should have (a/an/the/X) main role in supporting a family.

5. A man from one of these cultures might be unhappy with (a/an/the/X) working wife, especially one who earns more than the husband does.

6. In certain cultures, (a/an/the/X) wives are even considered the property of their husband's family.

7. (A/An/The/X) woman who would be unable to live in such a male-dominated household should avoid marrying a man from a culture that has very traditional views.

8. Some people, however, develop (a/an/the/X) interest in their new culture that is so strong that they are willing to leave their own traditions behind.

9. Many women embrace these new cultural aspects such as (a/an/the/X) music, clothing, and participation in cultural events.

10. In the end, many of the happiest cross-cultural marriages are those in which the couple finds (a/an/the/X) appropriate balance between their traditions.

Exercise 2.2 Articles

In each of the following sentences, cross out the italicized article if it is unnecessary or incorrect.

Example: ~~The~~ *M*any Americans disagree about prayer in public schools.

1. The U.S. Constitution guarantees freedom of *a* religion to all residents of the country.

2. The United States does not have *an* established state religion.

3. Instead, by *the* law, all residents are allowed to worship as they please or to choose not to worship at all.

4. The U.S. Supreme Court declared *the* school prayer unconstitutional about forty years ago.

5. As a result, many Americans were very unhappy with *the* Court's decision.

6. Students in American public schools are not forbidden to pray silently in class—for example, before *a* test.

7. Teachers or *the* other authority figures in a school may not legally lead prayers in class or at school functions.

8. Student religious organizations do have the right to meet as *an* extracurricular school club.

9. The U.S. Constitution does not restrict the practice of *the* personal religious beliefs.

10. But the law does not permit the use of *a* class time in public schools for group expression of *a* particular faith.

Exercise 2.3 Articles

In the sentences below, write **a**, **an**, or **the** in each blank.

Example: I waited in line for _____*an*_____ hour to set up my cell phone plan.

1. Cell phone usage in _____ United States has risen dramatically in the last four years.

2. There was _____ time when it seemed that only business people had mobile phones.

3. Mobile phones of _____ 1980s were bulky, heavy objects.

4. Cell phones of _____ new millennium are slim, sleek, and lightweight.

5. _____ cell phone used to cost hundreds of dollars, but now they are sometimes given away with service plans.

6. _____ few of my friends have given up their land lines in favor of using cell phones for all their calls.

7. There has been _____ drastic increase in usage among teenagers.

8. They believe that cell phones are _____ absolute necessity.

9. After all, maintaining _____ social life is important when you are sixteen years old.

10. The parents of _____ teenager would probably disagree.

Exercise 2.4 Articles

Revise each of the following sentences by adding, deleting, or changing articles wherever necessary.

Example: Footnotes at the bottom of a̶ *the* page give you more information.

1. It is surprising how many parts there are to a textbook.

2. Most students never read beyond first page of homework assignment in a textbook. But there are many useful parts to book.

3. For example, the preface is at the beginning of most books. This gives you information on how to use the book.

4. The table of contents is after the preface. It shows you the chapter, the subject, and the page number.

5. There is usually an appendix after the assignments that gives you useful information such as dictionary or glossary of terms used in the textbook.

6. At the end of the book, there is a index. This is an alphabetical list of all the topics in the book and their page number.

7. Some textbooks contain an answer key to the questions at the very back of the book.

8. Beyond the usual parts of a textbook, there may be charts to assist in understanding the subject matter.

9. Perhaps the most popular items contained within a book are the pictures.

10. In the end, it is still a textbook, and an only page that matters to the student is the homework assignment.

Exercise 2.5 Taking the Next Step with Articles

Write about the most exciting thing you've ever done. Where did it happen? Who was with you? Why was it exciting? Be sure to use the articles *a, an,* and *the* and words that use the zero article plus any new vocabulary. Refer to the relevant sections of this chapter as you work to help you master each concept.

_____

_____

_____

_____

_____

_____

_____

_____

_____

Part 3
Pronouns

Pronouns take the place of nouns, other pronouns, or phrases functioning as nouns. You can use them to avoid repetition of previously mentioned words. Pronouns must agree with the nouns they replace. Look for pronoun agreement with case, number, and gender. Examine the following examples:

All of the <u>students</u> brought **their** books to class.

Do you like <u>paintings</u> by Monet or **those** by Picasso?

<u>Jack</u> ate **his** lunch quickly.

Personal Pronouns

Pronouns that function as the subject of a sentence or clause are called **personal pronouns**. (These are also sometimes called subject pronouns.)

		Singular	Plural
First person		I	we
Second person		you	you
Third person	*masculine*	he	they
	feminine	she	
	neuter	it	

<u>Audrey</u> went to the store for eggs. **She**'ll be back shortly.

The red <u>scarf</u> hung on the coat rack where someone left **it** a long time ago.

Since **he** had been working indoors all afternoon, <u>Nicholas</u> needed some fresh air. (*pronoun precedes subject Nicholas*)

<u>Colin</u>, can **you** help me open this <u>window</u>? **It**'s stuck.

<u>Leanne and I</u> had planned to watch a movie, but **we** went swimming instead.

Object Pronouns

Pronouns that function as the object of a sentence or clause are called **object pronouns**.

		Singular	Plural
First person		me	us
Second person		you	you
Third person	*masculine*	him	them
	feminine	her	
	neuter	it	

Since <u>Tom</u> was going out in the rain, Cindy gave **him** the large umbrella.

<u>My cousins</u> are in town this week, so I'm going to the museum with **them**.

<u>That mud puddle</u> is deep. Don't step into **it**.

<u>The woman</u> in line at the post office let us go in front of **her**.

Possessive Pronouns

Pronouns in the **possessive case**, also called **possessive pronouns**, are used to show possession or ownership.

		Singular	Plural
First person		my/mine	our/ours
Second person		your/yours	your/yours
Third person	*masculine*	his	their/theirs
	feminine	her/hers	
	neuter	its	

<u>Nicholas</u>, you should buy this tie for **your** father.

The further <u>Julie</u> hiked, the heavier **her** backpack seemed.

<u>Mike</u> has to travel a lot for **his** job.

Our son just learned how to walk.

You should use the possessive pronouns *mine, yours* (singular), *hers, ours, yours* (plural), and *theirs* only after a helping verb. You can use *his* and *its* before a noun as well as after a helping verb.

This house is **hers**.	That's **her** house.
The fault is **mine**.	It's **my** fault.
Which car is **his**?	That's **his** car.
That's **yours**.	That's **your** wallet.

Note that while nouns use **apostrophes** to show possession, pronouns have their own special forms to show possession and do not use apostrophes. A pronoun with an apostrophe is a **contraction**, not a possessive pronoun. It is easy to confuse these forms because they are **homonyms** (words that are pronounced the same but spelled differently). Compare the following possessive pronouns with their homonym contractions.

Possessive pronouns	Contractions
its = belonging to it	it's = it is
your = belonging to you	you're = you are
their = belonging to them	they're = they are

Exercise 3.1 Personal Pronouns

Underline the correct pronoun from the pair in parentheses.

Example: Dogs that do not behave can be dangerous. (It/<u>They</u>) need communication, love, and training.

1. If (you/he) have a dog, it is a good idea to train it.

2. (You/He) should hire a trainer because your pet will be more responsive to a professional.

3. People are more likely to train dogs than cats. (They/You) believe dogs are easier to train.

4. A trainer teaches dogs to behave around strangers. Otherwise, (they/he) may bark, bite, or attack us.

5. Young children are especially at risk because (they/we) like to pet dogs, but owners want to make sure their dog won't harm them.

6. When (you/she) take your dog for a walk, you will probably put a leash on it.

7. (We/They) take our dogs for long walks, and sometimes they wrap their leashes around us.

8. One of our dogs is female, and (he/I) love taking her on long walks.

9. Both of our dogs let children rub their bellies, and (they/he) love licking the children's faces.

10. (They/She) don't even mind when our cats play with their doggy toys.

Exercise 3.2 Personal Pronouns

In each sentence, choose which pronoun should be inserted into the blank space provided. Choose from the following list: *he, she, it,* or *they*.

Example: Amazon.com was one of the first companies to sell items on the Internet. The history of _____*it*_____ is quite fascinating.

1. Jeff Bezos founded Amazon.com in 1994. Some claim that his idea for the company came while sitting in his van when _____ was moving to Seattle, Washington.

2. The story says that as Bezos's wife was driving the car, _____ typed up the business plan for the company on his laptop.

3. When _____ arrived in Seattle, Bezos started the business from his garage. _____ also started a basic Web site through which he could make sales.

4. Amazon.com sold only books online at first. Books were popular, and _____ were easy to ship.

5. Bezos hired various people to help with technical details of his online business. His wife helped with nontechnical matters. _____ has contributed to the company since its early days.

6. Bezos realized that _____ had to expand his selection of items in order to grow his business. If he sold only books, the company would not be able to grow.

7. In 1997, Amazon.com started selling CDs as well as books. The company became very popular, its sales grew tremendously, and _____ experienced an increase in profits.

8. In 1998, Amazon.com began to sell computer software, electronics, toys, and home improvement selections. Bezos had started a large company, and _____ was experiencing success.

9. However, the economy suffered in 2001, and the "dot.com" bust occurred. Amazon.com's sales declined significantly. Bezos had to lay off over a thousand workers, and _____ needed to rethink his strategy.

10. Bezos created a new business plan and Amazon.com recovered. The company's sales increased. _____ is now one of the largest online retail sites.

Exercise 3.3 Personal Pronouns

For each of the following sentences, fill in the blank with the correct pronoun.

> **Example:** "The Star Spangled Banner" is the national anthem of the United States. Americans are proud, and _____*they*_____ sing it before every baseball game.

1. Francis Scott Key, a lawyer in Georgetown, wrote the national anthem of the United States more than 200 years ago. _____ is still sung today.

2. The song inspires many Americans. _____ place their right hands over their hearts when they sing it.

3. The anthem has a challenging melody, so _____ isn't easy to sing.

4. If _____ forget the lyrics, people will often hum along.

5. _____ have the lyrics memorized in our household.

6. _____ get emotional when I hear the anthem; it moves me to tears.

7. When we hear the national anthems of other nations, _____ also mean something to us.

8. When the national anthem is sung before sporting events, _____ is meant as a reminder.

9. A famous female singer performed the anthem at Super Bowl XLIII. _____ did a fantastic job and earned a round of applause from the crowd.

10. Francis Scott Key wrote a beautiful anthem, and _____ would be proud to know just how often it is sung.

Exercise 3.4 Object Pronouns

Underline the correct pronoun from the pair in parentheses.

Example: *The Odyssey* is a Greek poem written by Homer. (<u>It</u>/They) was written in 80 B.C.

1. *The Odyssey* is the story of King Odysseus and his travels after the Trojan War. From the beginning of the epic poem, there are powerful forces working against (her/him).

2. Odysseus is twenty years old when he leaves his homeland, the island of Ithaca, and forty years old before he sees (it/them) again.

3. Odysseus is married to Penelope, and he leaves (him/her) behind to raise their son, Telemachus.

4. Penelope believes that Odysseus will come home after the war is over, but she is unaware of the gods' plots to delay (her/him).

5. The war lasts for ten years, and it takes Odysseus another ten years to return to (her/him).

6. During the war, the Greeks fight to bring down the city of Troy, and eventually they do conquer (it/them).

7. Many warriors are killed on both sides, including Achilles, a warrior known for his awful temper. Paris is the one who finally kills (her/him).

8. Odysseus helps win the war with his cunning. The Greeks would not have won (it/them) without him.

9. On his way home, he encounters many situations that delay (him/her).

10. When the weary king finally returns to the people of Ithaca, he is overjoyed to see (them/us).

Exercise 3.5 Object Pronouns

For each of the following sentences, fill in the blank with the correct pronoun.

Example: An arranged marriage need not be as negative as _____*it*_____ sounds. There can be examples of instant attraction.

1. Arranged marriages are still a cultural norm in India. The prospective bride and groom are often not opposed to _____ when they both want to adhere to traditional customs.

2. While many couples arrange marriages with the partners they choose, sometimes the couples' elders arrange _____ .

3. The man's family might send photographs of _____ to the woman's family.

4. The woman's family plays an important role in arranging for eligible bachelors to meet _____ .

5. At the first meeting, the bachelor may talk about his education, family background, or potential for future success. The woman and her family will want to know about all of _____ .

6. If the man and the woman seem suitable for marriage, the parents might arrange _____ right away.

7. If you didn't grow up in a culture with arranged marriages, you might not like having your spouse chosen for _____ .

8. My parents had an arranged marriage, but when I started dating they agreed not to arrange one for _____ .

9. They did not force their views on my sister or _____ ; in fact, they respect our different views of marriage.

10. Both types of marriage can succeed if the couple remembers their vows and succeeds in honoring _____ .

Exercise 3.6 Object Pronouns

For each of the following sentences, fill in the blank with the correct pronoun.

Example: I bought all the textbooks I needed for my classes, but I got sick the first day
and missed _____*them*_____ .

1. When I started college, I had no idea how much the college lifestyle would change
   _____ .

2. I went to the state university my first year of college. Then I considered other schools
   and started finding information about _____ .

3. An advantage of attending a state university is that _____ is more affordable than a private university.

4. During my second year, I discovered a state college that seemed more suitable for
   _____ .

5. The folks at the admissions office sent _____ a promotional brochure
   about the school, and I knew _____ was the college for me.

6. After I was accepted, my dad drove _____ to the campus. I was glad to
   have _____ with me.

7. I thought the college campus was beautiful. _____ had green rolling hills
   and towering trees.

8. The first girl I met was also new, and she became my best friend. I helped
   _____ get through the next few years.

9. My father had tears in his eyes as he watched _____ accept my diploma.

10. My graduation happened more than ten years ago, but my father still talks about
    _____ .

Exercise 3.7 Possessive Pronouns

Underline the correct pronoun from the pair in parentheses.

Example: "If you have a good song, you can't escape (<u>its</u>/their) beauty," Ray Charles said.

1. Ray Charles was a pioneer of the music industry who influenced many other musicians with (its/his) music.

2. He was born in Georgia and later moved with (his/her) small family to northern Florida.

3. He and his brother didn't know their father, and Ray's mother raised both of (her/his) sons alone.

4. His mother worked as a laborer to provide as much for (their/her) sons as she could.

5. Ray Charles witnessed his brother's death, and that memory haunted him throughout (his/our) entire life.

6. Ray Charles started losing his vision when he was five years old, but he adjusted to (its/her) absence and continued pursuing (his/her) passion for music.

7. He went to a school for the blind in St. Augustine, where he developed (their/his) technical skills on the piano.

8. He listened to Nat King Cole and Charles Brown, and (his/their) influence is evident in his earlier recordings.

9. He influenced artists in jazz, but many artists in country, gospel, and soul also owe (his/their) success to Ray Charles.

10. He has said that classical music is European but that jazz is (their/our) music, meaning it was born in America and belongs to Americans.

Exercise 3.8 Possessive Pronouns

Underline the correct pronoun from the pair in parentheses.

> **Example:** Prior to becoming president, Jimmy Carter was a peanut farmer. (Its/<u>His</u>) family farm was well known across the United States.

1. Jimmy Carter served as president of the United States from 1977 to 1981, but he is known more for (her/his) peacemaking work after his presidency than for (her/his) domestic work during that time.

2. He and his wife Rosalynn moved to the White House with (their/our) young daughter, Amy.

3. Amy was only ten years old when she left (her/my) hometown of Plains, Georgia.

4. Before becoming president, Jimmy Carter served as the governor of (his/its) state.

5. After his presidency, Jimmy Carter founded the Carter Center, which is guided by (their/his) principles of social justice.

6. Rosalynn Carter helps (my/her) husband manage the Carter Center.

7. In addition to working with him, she devotes time to other of (her/our) favorite causes.

8. The Carters also volunteer for Habitat for Humanity, an organization that helps people build (their/our) own homes.

9. President Carter received the Nobel Peace Prize for (her/his) work promoting peace and economic development throughout the world.

10. President Carter will be remembered in America as one of (its/our) greatest citizens.

Exercise 3.9 Possessive Pronouns

Fill in each blank with the correct possessive pronoun.

> **Example:** I put _____*my*_____ clothes in a paper bag and moved with my mother to the United States.

I first came to the United States when I was five years old to live with

(1.) _____ father. My mother and I left our home in 1973, and it changed

(2.) _____ lives forever. My mother was anxious about leaving

(3.) _____ mother and father and my sister behind. My father missed

(4.) _____ own mother and father at first, but he adjusted to living by himself.

My sister moved to the United States two years later to complete (5.) _____

family reunion.

Initially, I was too shy to talk to (6.) _____ teacher and classmates.

Eventually, I overcame my timid ways and played just like all the other children in

(7.) _____ class.

I have lived in the United States for over twenty-five years, but I still practice some

traditions from (8.) _____ native culture. Most children learn about traditions

from (9.) _____ parents; I learned how to cook from my mother. I only hope

that (10.) _____ own children learn something about our culture from me.

Exercise 3.10 Object/Possessive Pronouns

Underline the correct object or possessive pronoun from the pair in parentheses.

> **Example:** For many men and women across America, golf is (them/<u>their</u>) number-one recreational sport.

1. Golf is a sport that challenges players to perfect (their/them) skills.

2. At the very least, golfers need clubs, golf balls, and gloves to make (their/them) game the best it can be.

3. If I were an amateur golfer, I might take (my/me) clubs to a golf course and hit a few balls to warm up.

4. Professional golfers play for money, so (them/their) equipment is very important to (them/their).

5. Annika Sorenstam plays every hole with great intensity. Her skill impresses (me/my).

6. Tiger Woods is a golfer who executes (his/him) shots with exceptional grace and skill.

7. I enjoy watching a close competition, even if the sport itself bores (me/my).

8. Golf tournaments are often broadcast on television, but they are too boring for (me/my) taste.

9. The most exciting way to experience golf is to watch (it/its) firsthand at a tournament.

10. If you go to a golf tournament, don't forget to bring (you/your) umbrella and sunscreen.

Exercise 3.11 Object/Possessive Pronouns

Fill in each blank with the correct object or possessive pronoun.

> **Example:** Once, in high school, there was a friend of _____*mine*_____ who greatly
> upset me over a class assignment.

1. One day I was eating my lunch at school when my friend Jared asked me for help. He
   was in _____ history class.

2. He told _____ that he had not read the assigned reading chapter for
   class. He wanted me to tell _____ the main points of the chapter before
   _____ class that day.

3. I told him, "I will give _____ my notes that I took while reading the
   chapter. However, please return them to me when we get to class. They are
   _____."

4. Jared said, "Thanks! You can count on _____. I'll return _____."

5. When I got to class, I did not see _____. All of the other students were
   in their seats, and our teacher began asking _____ questions about
   the chapter.

6. She called on me and asked _____ a question about a Civil War battle.
   I gave _____ the answer; I knew it even without my notes.

7. But I was still not happy with Jared. I was a bit angry with _____.

8. When class ended, I walked out and found Jared in the parking lot. I asked
   _____ why he had not attended class. He told _____ that
   he was afraid to come to class because he had not read the chapter.

9. I told _____ that he should plan his time better. I said that next time
   we could read the chapter together and take notes. Then the notes would be
   _____, not just mine.

10. He thought this plan sounded great. "I like _____! This will help me better
    prepare for the next class!"

Exercise 3.12 Object/Possessive Pronouns

Fill in the blanks in the paragraphs below with the correct object or possessive pronoun.

Example: Good doctors care about their patients and will treat _____*them*_____ with respect and professionalism.

Doctors are caring people who are genuinely concerned about (1.) _____

patients' health. Some doctors work in hospitals while others have (2.) _____

own practices. Our family doctor is Dr. Tate Rockwell, and I trust (3.) _____

completely. His wife, Marcy, is also a doctor. He helped (4.) _____ set up a

private practice a block away so that she would be working nearby.

My former doctor's office was always busy. Even when his patients didn't have appoint-

ments, he never refused to see (5.) _____ . He didn't share his practice with

other doctors because they couldn't tolerate (6.) _____ policies. When choos-

ing a physician, you should find a doctor whose philosophy on treatment closely matches

(7.) _____ own. This way, you will be satisfied with the health care he provides

for (8.) _____ . Otherwise, you could be disappointed with the treatment

options offered by (9.) _____ doctor. Good doctors maintain strict schedules

because it helps (10.) _____ make sure that (11.) _____ patients

receive treatment in a timely manner.

Reflexive and Intensive Pronouns

Reflexive and intensive pronouns have the same forms but function differently. Reflexive pronouns refer back to the subject of the sentence in which they occur. Intensive pronouns have the same form as reflexive pronouns and are used to emphasize their subject.

First person		myself	ourselves
Second person		yourself	yourself
Third person	*masculine*	himself (<u>never</u> hisself)	themselves
	feminine	herself	
	neuter	itself	

Reflexive pronouns	<u>I</u> try not to take **myself** too seriously.
	<u>The boss</u> gave **himself** a raise.
	<u>You</u> should be good to **yourself**.
Intensive pronouns	<u>We</u> installed this carpet **ourselves**.
	<u>The professor</u> **herself** acknowledged the student's achievement.
	<u>The president of the company</u> **himself** came to the airport to pick up the guests.

Notice that intensive pronouns can be left out of a sentence and the sentence will still make sense, although there will no longer be any emphasis. But removing a reflexive pronoun makes the sentence incomplete.

Intensive	**Correct**	<u>We</u> installed this carpet **ourselves**.
	Correct	We installed this carpet.
Reflexive	**Correct**	<u>You</u> should be good to **yourself**.
	Incorrect	You should be good to.

Be aware that the expression *by* + intensive pronoun or *all by* + intensive pronoun is idiomatic and typically indicates that no other person was involved in the action specified.

We built the shelves **by ourselves**.

Julie made those curtains **all by herself**.

Also, pay attention to the phrase *talking to oneself* and its variants. It is a common expression in English, and it involves a reflexive pronoun.

He assembled the cabinet while **talking to himself** the entire time.

She **told herself** not to make the same mistake again.

He **grumbled to himself** as he wrote a letter of complaint to the manager.

Relative Pronouns

The relative pronouns *who, whom, whose, which,* and *that* link dependent clauses to independent clauses to form complete sentences from two separate ideas. When choosing a relative pronoun, it is important to understand the difference between **restrictive** and **nonrestrictive** clauses. Restrictive clauses contain information crucial to the main idea of the sentence. They cannot be removed without changing the sentence's meaning and they are *not* set off from the rest of the sentence by commas. Nonrestrictive clauses can be left out of a sentence without changing the main idea; they *are* set off from the rest of the sentence by commas. (For more information on clauses, go to Part 5.)

That/Which

In restrictive clauses, use *that* to refer to animals or things. In nonrestrictive clauses, use *which* to refer to animals or things.

Restrictive clause	The hawk **that was my uncle's pet** was named Tootsie.
Nonrestrictive clause	The hawk, **which had been flying low over the ground**, swooped down to catch a mouse in its talons.
Restrictive clause	The film **that my aunt recommended** turned out to be very entertaining.
Nonrestrictive clause	That film, **which is still showing in the theaters**, is very unusual.

In restrictive and nonrestrictive clauses, use *who*, *whom*, or *whose* (depending on the function of the pronoun in the dependent clause) to refer to people.

Who

Use *who* when the relative pronoun functions as the subject of the dependent clause.

Restrictive clause	The person **who lives in that brick house** has many kinds of pets.
Nonrestrictive clause	My neighbor, **who lives in that brick house**, adopted a kitten from the animal shelter.

Whom

In formal writing, use *whom* when the relative pronoun functions as the object of the dependent clause. But be aware that in many cases English speakers use *who* or *that* in place of *whom*. When choosing whether to use *whom*, *who*, or *that*, think about the occasion for writing and who will be reading your writing. *Whom* can sound awkward or pretentious in casual contexts, such as in conversation or e-mail. But *whom* may be a better choice for more formal academic writing. Consult your instructor if you are not sure.

Formal

Restrictive clause	That literature professor **whom everyone knows and loves** is retiring this year.
Nonrestrictive clause	Our professor, **whom the university awarded an honorary degree**, is revered by all.

Informal

Restrictive clause	The customer **who I waited on** was rude.
or	The customer **that I waited on** was rude.
Nonrestrictive clause	The customer, **who we recognized from two days ago**, asked for more coffee.

Whose

Use *whose* when the relative pronoun functions as the possessive pronoun.

Restrictive clause	The man **whose dog ran away** is offering a reward for finding it.
Nonrestrictive clause	My neighbor, **whose dog ran away recently**, is building a fence around his yard.

Exercise 3.13 Reflexive/Intensive Pronouns

Underline the correct pronoun from the pair in parentheses.

> **Example:** Tired of waiting for her husband to help in the kitchen, the woman sharpened the knife (itself/<u>herself</u>).

1. The woman cut (herself/yourself) while chopping vegetables.

2. Her husband drove her to the hospital (itself/himself).

3. She didn't want to drive (themselves/herself), so she was glad that he volunteered.

4. At the hospital, they sat by (themselves/ourselves) until the nurse took them to see the doctor.

5. The doctor was a young man who worked by (himself/herself) in the evenings.

6. He asked the woman, "How did you hurt (himself/yourself)?"

7. She said, "I'm usually careful with a knife. I've never done this to (myself/herself) before."

8. He said the cut wasn't bad and would require only a few stitches. He did the stitching (yourself/himself).

9. He asked if they needed a ride home, but the couple replied, "We drove here (themselves/ourselves)."

10. The doctor wished them well and said, "I hope you both will take good care of (yourselves/themselves)."

Exercise 3.14 Reflexive/Intensive Pronouns

Underline the correct pronoun from the pair in parentheses.

Example: Upon meeting them, people will present (himself/<u>themselves</u>) as the perfect roommate until you live with them.

1. People who live together have to live by rules. They make up the rules (themselves/ itself).

2. In college, I had several roommates, but I always wanted to live by (ourselves/myself).

3. My first roommate was a girl who didn't like to do anything (herself/himself).

4. Our one rule was that we were to always clean up after (ourselves/themselves).

5. My second roommate situation was with two girls and one guy. Until I moved in, they lived by (ourselves/themselves) in a big house.

6. The guy liked to cook for (herself/himself); the rest of us didn't know how to cook.

7. One girl worked at a bank to put (himself/herself) through college.

8. My last living situation was the best: I finally got to live by (myself/itself).

9. When living alone, one has only (oneself/myself) to blame if things are not right.

10. Still, I enjoyed living alone; I only had to make rules for (herself/myself).

Exercise 3.15 Reflexive/Intensive Pronouns

Underline the correct pronoun from the pair in parentheses.

Example: Sarah was a child of the 1970s who rallied her friends to make changes for (themselves/herself).

1. When Sarah was in college, she was unhappy with the student government. She thought, "If I want things to be better, I will have to do something about it (himself/myself)."

2. She decided to run for student president (herself/itself).

3. She recruited several friends to campaign for her around campus; they even put the posters up (yourselves/themselves).

4. Although her friends helped put up the posters, Sarah knew she had to write her campaign speech (herself/myself).

5. One of her opponents was a fellow named John; he told her (herself/himself) that she would make a good president.

6. Sarah's speech slogan was, "If we want to make our lives better, we have to do it (yourselves/ourselves)."

7. After listening to all the speeches, students decided for (ourselves/themselves) which candidate would best represent them.

8. The voting took place on Thursday afternoon; Sarah voted for (herself/myself).

9. Mr. Smith, the president of the college, counted the votes (itself/himself).

10. On Friday, it was announced that Sarah had won the election. She said, "I'm so happy, I don't know what to say for (myself/herself)."

Exercise 3.16 Relative Pronouns

Fill in the blank with the correct relative pronoun.

Example: Charlie had never had a party before _____*that*_____ everyone enjoyed. He was nervous.

1. Charlie wanted to have a party for all of his friends, but he wasn't sure _____ to invite.

2. He asked his girlfriend, Lisa, about the guest list, but she just said, "You should invite the friends _____ you like."

3. He picked Saturday night because it was a night _____ would work for his friends.

4. Charlie also wanted to have the party in the backyard, _____ was so beautiful when the weather was good.

5. A few days before the party, he started to plan the menu, _____ consisted of simple but tasty appetizers.

6. He realized that most people would come hungry, so he decided to provide food _____ would satisfy them.

7. He had also thought of a theme for the party, _____ he kept secret until the day of the event.

8. He bought drinks and paper supplies, _____ all matched his theme.

9. After all the guests _____ had been invited arrived, Charlie revealed the theme of the party: a marriage proposal.

10. The guest for _____ he had planned the party was pleasantly surprised when he asked her to marry him.

Exercise 3.17 Relative Pronouns

Fill in the blank with the correct relative pronoun.

Example: When there is a car sale, it is difficult to know _____*which*_____ car really is the best deal.

1. When Jake decided to buy a car, he didn't know _____ one to buy.

2. He also didn't know _____ to take with him to the dealership.

3. Jake did know _____ he wanted a car that was both affordable and stylish.

4. Jake and his friend, Tom, went to the car dealership _____ came the most highly recommended.

5. All of the salespeople seemed nice, but Jake and Tom still didn't know _____ they trusted most.

6. The first car Jake saw was a compact car _____ was exactly the right size, but he also thought it looked rather plain.

7. The next car, _____ was the most expensive, was roomier and had a sun roof.

8. But the car _____ Jake really wanted was a small sports car.

9. The saleswoman said, "If I know _____ the car is for, I can make a better recommendation."

10. Finally, Jake found the one _____ was right for him: a used sports car with a sun roof.

Exercise 3.18 Relative Pronouns

Combine the two sentences by using a relative pronoun. Be sure to add a comma before any nonrestrictive clauses, where necessary.

Example: The Taj Mahal has a large white marble and tile dome, *which* It is the most famous piece of the structure.

1. The Taj Mahal is a monument. It is considered one of the most beautiful sites in the world.

2. The Taj Mahal is a memorial. King Shah Jahan built it for his queen, Mumtaz Mahal.

3. It is also an ancient mausoleum. It holds the tomb of Mumtaz Mahal.

4. King Shah Jahan wanted to show his deep love for Mumtaz Mahal. She died during childbirth.

5. The King decreed that the Taj Mahal be built in a special location. It had to be both scenic and close to his palace.

6. The King wanted to build a monument. No one would ever forget it.

7. Shah Jahan selected skilled architects and masons. They came from all over India and the Middle East.

8. The Taj Mahal is made of marble, precious stones, and gems. These materials made it a very expensive project.

9. Every year the Taj Mahal attracts millions of visitors. They are always surprised at the grandeur and size of the monument.

10. The Taj Mahal is an extraordinary monument. It is a testimony to the deep love Shah Jahan had for his wife.

Exercise 3.19 Taking the Next Step with Pronouns

Write about a person who has been significant in your life. He or she might be a parent, sibling, or another relative; or he or she might be a teacher, coach, or friend. When you use pronouns in this description, be sure to use the masculine and feminine forms correctly.

_____

_____

_____

_____

_____

_____

_____

_____

_____

Part 4
Negative Statements and Questions

Negative Statements

There are several guidelines to follow in forming negative statements.

1. Add the adverb *not*.

2. Add a helping verb before *not* if one is not already present in the original sentence. If a helping verb is present, it should be placed immediately in front of *not*. (See p. 87 for a definition of helping verbs.)

3. If a helping verb must be added, change the main verb to the base form.

> John is leaving for New York tomorrow morning.
> John is **not** leaving for New York tomorrow morning.
>
> John will take the 6:40 A.M. flight.
> John will **not** take the 6:40 A.M. flight.
>
> John likes to fly.
> John does **not** like to fly.
>
> John checked his luggage at the gate.
> John did **not** check his luggage at the gate.

Questions

Yes/No Questions

Simple yes/no questions, often called **closed questions**, are questions that you can answer with just a yes or a no (or their equivalent).

Follow the steps below to form yes/no questions from declarative sentences that already contain a "be" verb (*am, is, are*):

1. Switch the position of the subject and the "be" verb so that the helping verb comes first in the sentence.

2. Replace the period with a question mark.

> He is tired and hungry.
> **Is** he tired and hungry**?**
>
> We are staying in a motel tonight.
> **Are** we staying in a motel tonight**?**
>
> They were upset.
> **Were** they upset**?**

Follow the steps below to form yes/no questions from declarative sentences that do not contain a "be" verb:

1. Add the verb *do* in the appropriate tense in front of the subject, making sure it agrees with the subject.

2. Change the main verb to its base form.

3. Replace the period with a question mark.

> I said I would go.
> **Did** I **say** I would go**?**
>
> She starts her new job on Monday.
> **Does** she **start** her new job on Monday**?**
>
> We know our team's score.
> **Do** we **know** our team's score**?**

Open Questions

In English, if information other than yes or no is desired, question words are used. Sometimes they are called the **wh- words**: *who, whom, what, which, whose, where, when, why, how*. The kinds of questions formed with question words are often called **open questions**. As with yes/no questions, they usually require a helping verb. However, the question word must come before the helping verb.

> He went to the dentist yesterday. **Who** went to the dentist yesterday?
> **Where** did he go yesterday?
> **Why** did he go to the dentist?
> **How** did he go to the dentist?
> **When** did he go to the dentist?
> **Which** dentist did he go to? (informal)
> To **which** dentist did he go? (formal)
> **What** time did he go to the dentist?

In many cases, you can make an open question from a yes/no question simply by adding the appropriate question word in front of the question.

Declarative sentence	You took the bus.
Yes/no question	**Did** you **take** the bus?
Open questions	**When** did you take the bus?
	Where did you take the bus?
	Why did you take the bus?

In the following questions, notice that when the question word asks about the subject of the sentence, there is no need for a helping verb. When the question asks about the object of a sentence, you must change the word order and use a form of *do*.

Subject questions	Object questions
Who took my pencil?	What did you take?
Whose dog bit my brother?	Whom did the dog bite? (formal)
	Who did the dog bite? (informal)
Which car won the race?	Which race did the car win?
What kind of mammal lays eggs?	What do baby mammals eat?

Using the wh- words, we can create the following questions from the sentence below.

Rich quickly ran to the convenience store on the corner this morning to buy cough medicine for his sister Leslie.

Question	Answer
Who ran to the store?	**Rich** ran to the store.
What did he buy?	He bought **medicine**.
What kind of medicine?	He bought **cough** medicine.
Why did he go to the store?	He went **to buy cough medicine**.
When did he go to the store?	He went **this morning**.
How did he run to the store?	He ran **quickly**.
Where was the store?	The store was **on the corner**.
For **whom** did he buy the medicine?	He bought the medicine **for his sister Leslie**.
or **Who** did he buy the medicine for?	He bought the medicine **for his sister Leslie**.
Whose sister is Leslie?	She is **Rich's** sister.
To **which** store did he run?	He ran to the **convenience** store.
or **Which** store did he run to?	or He ran to the store **on the corner**.

Exercise 4.1 Negative Statements

Form negative statements from the regular sentences by changing the verb.

Example: Kanji characters ~~are~~ *are not* difficult when you practice the beautiful flow of these ancient symbols.

1. In my first year of college, most of my friends chose to study one of the romance languages.

2. More recently, languages such as Chinese or Japanese have been more popular.

3. Studying a new language in the early morning has been satisfying.

4. I learned several thousand kanji characters.

5. Learning the kanji characters also helped me learn Japanese.

6. The Japanese language uses kanji characters in its written language.

7. I practiced speaking Chinese with native speakers at my college.

8. They said that they understood me.

9. I believed they were telling me the truth.

10. I loved learning and speaking another language.

Exercise 4.2 Negative Statements

Form negative statements from the regular sentences by changing the verb. You may need to change other words in the sentence as well.

Example: The company that I work for ~~allows~~ *does not allow* telecommuting.

1. Telecommuting, which refers to working at home, is supported by my boss.

2. My boss allows every employee in our company to telecommute at least one day per week.

3. Traffic in our area is very bad, and telecommuting is needed to help reduce the number of cars on the road.

4. My boss feels that telecommuting improves the attitude of employees.

5. He also thinks that if employees' attitudes are good, they will work harder.

6. Therefore, my boss believes that telecommuting results in higher productivity.

7. My boss allows some employees to telecommute more than one day a week.

8. He allows some employees to telecommute more than one day because some employees live far away from our office.

9. My boss thinks that in the future every employee will work from home almost every day of the week.

10. I like my boss because he allows telecommuting.

Exercise 4.3 Negative Statements

Form negative statements from the regular sentences by changing the verb.

      did not want
  Example: People ~~wanted~~ to fly because they were afraid of being so high above the
      safe ground.

1. Before the invention of the modern airplane, people traveled by car or railway.

2. People owned only one car for road trips.

3. Better highways were constructed as more and more people traveled by car.

4. The railway provided an alternate mode of traveling.

5. Railway trains offered luxury accommodations such as sleeping cabins and fine restaurants.

6. People also found a way to travel overseas: luxury cruise ships.

7. Cruise ship operators took into account the length of the journey in their plans.

8. Airlines also began offering luxury accommodations such as first-class seats and hot meals on flights.

9. Some airlines even have fully reclining seats and televisions for each passenger.

10. Perhaps one day there will be gyms on airplanes!

Exercise 4.4 Negative Statements

Form negative statements from the regular sentences by changing the verb.

did not have

Example: Van Gogh ~~had~~ a good relationship with his mother and father.
                    ∧

1. Van Gogh learned to paint as a young man.

2. His paintings can be seen in museums around the world.

3. He is best known for his textured brush strokes.

4. He painted with oil paints to produce rich scenes of nature.

5. Van Gogh was close to his brother, Theo.

6. He suffered from depression and an addiction to absinthe, a strong herbal liqueur.

7. Those two afflictions made his paintings more intense.

8. He died just around the time his artwork was becoming famous.

9. Many collectors and museums have bought his paintings.

10. Van Gogh's famous painting of sunflowers sold for millions of dollars.

Exercise 4.5 Questions

Read each statement and form a question that would be answered by the statement.

Example: Ringo Starr and Paul McCartney continue to record music today.

Answer: *Who continues to record music today?*

1. The Beatles were from Liverpool, England.

   _____

2. There were four musicians in the band.

   _____

3. Paul McCartney and John Lennon wrote many of the songs.

   _____

4. The band's first successful single was "Love Me Do."

   _____

5. The term for the crazed obsession with the Beatles is "Beatlemania."

   _____

6. The band performed on the *Ed Sullivan Show* in the United States in February 1964.

   _____

7. They also starred in the movie *A Hard Day's Night*.

   _____

8. John Lennon's wife's name was Yoko Ono.

   _____

9. The band's last performance was in San Francisco.

   _____

10. The band officially broke up in 1970.

   _____

Exercise 4.6 Questions

Change the following sentences into yes/no questions.

Example: Business Law is an exciting field of study.

Answer: *Is Business Law an exciting field of study?*

1. My cousin graduated from law school on Saturday.

   _____

2. His area of concentration is Business Law.

   _____

3. His undergraduate degree was in history.

   _____

4. He chose history because it seemed like a good pre-law degree.

   _____

5. There were 150 students who graduated with him.

   _____

6. The law school is located in southern Florida.

   _____

7. He plans to take the bar exam in July.

   _____

8. He would like to move to Washington, D.C.

   _____

9. He plans to move with his best friend.

   _____

10. He wants to live in Washington, D.C., because it has so many opportunities.

   _____

Exercise 4.7 Questions

Read each statement, and form a question that would be answered by the statement.

Example: A world-renowned runner carries the Olympic torch.

Answer: *Who carries the Olympic torch?* or *What does a world-renowned runner carry?*

1. The summer Olympics takes place every four years.

   _____

2. It features sporting events such as swimming, running, weightlifting, and gymnastics.

   _____

3. Athletes who represent their countries compete for gold, silver, or bronze medals.

   _____

4. The summer Olympics of 2008 took place in Beijing.

   _____

5. The first modern Olympic Games took place in 1892.

   _____

6. The decathlon consists of ten events, including the hurdles, the high jump, the discus throw, and the pole vault.

   _____

7. The marathon, a main event of the Olympics, is a 26-mile race.

   _____

8. The United States boycotted the Olympics in 1980 because of a political conflict with the former Soviet Union.

   _____

9. The Soviet Union boycotted the Olympics in 1984 because the United States boycotted in 1980.

   _____

10. The Olympic flag is made up of five rings to represent the five continents.

    _____

Exercise 4.8 Questions

Read each statement, and form a question that would be answered by the statement.

Example: An Academy Award is a prestigious honor for actors.

Answer: *What is a prestigious honor for actors?* _____

1. The motion picture industry has an awards ceremony called the Academy Awards.

   _____

2. The awards ceremony was created to recognize artists who had done exceptional work in the past year.

   _____

3. The ceremony takes place in Los Angeles, California.

   _____

4. The awards ceremony usually takes place in February.

   _____

5. Millions of viewers around the world see the ceremony on TV.

   _____

6. Celebrities wear beautiful gowns and tuxedos to the ceremony.

   _____

7. The most popular categories are best picture, best director, best actor, and best actress.

   _____

8. *The Lord of the Rings* won ten awards in 2004.

   _____

9. Jack Nicholson has won the most awards for a male actor in Academy history.

   _____

10. The Academy Awards are becoming more famous for the red carpet fashions.

   _____

Exercise 4.9 Taking the Next Step with Negative Statements and Questions

Write a comparison of your life now with your life five years ago. How have your habits changed (habits of eating, speaking, socializing, working, things you like to do)? Have your hopes for the future changed? This exercise will give you the opportunity to practice the skill of creating negative statements and using questions. Be sure to include both yes/no and open questions. Share this assignment with a classmate.

_____

_____

_____

_____

_____

_____

_____

_____

_____

Part 5
Sentences and Clauses

Sentence Subjects

In English, the most basic sentences (called **simple sentences**) require a subject and a verb. While in some informal writing and speech you may occasionally omit the subject, in most cases English requires you to state the subject. (Remember that imperative sentences have an implicit *you* as subject: [*You*] Return these books to the library.) Even when no true subject exists, English requires a "dummy" or "empty" subject to fill the subject position. *There* and *it* are commonly used as dummy subjects.

> **There** is enough food for everyone.

> **It** is cold out today.

You must also explicitly state the objects of sentences, even when they are understood.

> He threw the dog **a bone**.
> (not just *He threw*—even if the direct object *bone* and indirect object *dog* are obvious)

> Susan wants **that dress**.
> (not just *wants* or *Susan wants*—even if *Susan* and *dress* are clear from the context of the situation)

Word Order in Sentences

Be careful not to move subjects, verbs, or objects out of their normal positions in English sentences. English usually requires **subject-verb-object** word order. While there is some freedom regarding placement of adverbs, in general you should not separate the verb and its object.

> **Correct**   We **bought a large pizza** for dinner.
> **Incorrect**   We **bought** for dinner **a large pizza**.

Be aware that you may find instances of inverted word order in older English writing or poetry.

Exercise 5.1 Sentence Subjects

For each of the following sentences, underline the appropriate subject from the choices in parentheses. **X** means "no subject necessary."

> **Example:** (It/<u>There</u>/X) is much difference of opinion in the United States about the effects of television on young viewers.

1. Television (it/there/X) is available to almost everyone in the United States.

2. (It/There/X) is almost impossible to avoid television in some public places.

3. Some people believe that (it/there/X) is important for television programs to be constructive.

4. In particular, they argue that (it/there/X) is essential for children to receive positive messages from television.

5. (It/There/X) is much popular support for the idea that violent television shows can harm young viewers.

6. However, (it/there/X) is also true that many adults enjoy violent or graphic programs.

7. Many Americans believe that the media (it/there/X) is not to blame for how we use the information it presents.

8. (It/There/X) are ways for individuals to use media information wisely, many people say.

9. Many Americans argue that (it/there/X) is up to parents or guardians to make sure that children do not watch inappropriate television shows.

10. Most Americans seem to feel that (it/there/X) should not be government censorship of television programs.

Exercise 5.2 Word Order in Sentences

Revise each of the following sentences so that the verb is in the appropriate position.

Example: Most Americans ~~government censorship~~ (don't want)

1. Many people that too much sex and violence is shown on television believe.

2. Would like most parents to monitor their children's television viewing.

3. For many people, however, keeping track of a child's choice of television programs impossible is.

4. One solution might from recent technological innovations come.

5. Several years ago, agreed American television manufacturers to start equipping all new televisions with a V-chip.

6. The V for "violence" stands.

7. The V-chip out screens shows that contain sex and violence.

8. Parents the chip program to block shows with certain ratings.

9. With the V-chip, censor individuals, not the government, their children's television programs.

10. Of course, today, many children better than their parents know how to program electronic devices.

Exercise 5.3 Word Order in Sentences

Revise each of the following sentences so that subjects, verbs, and objects are in the correct English word order.

Example: Are there several problems with the V-chip system.

1. The television industry ratings for television programs provides so that parents can decide what to allow their children to watch.

2. The ratings system similar is to the one used for movies.

3. The ratings system exists already, but people get a V-chip only when they a new television buy.

4. Older children might to programming rated as explicit be attracted.

5. Most parents know that want kids what they are not allowed to have.

6. Parents with an older television shows rated for mature audiences will not be able to block out.

7. Say some critics that it is only a matter of time before a child learns to tamper with the V-chip programmer.

8. Advertisers worry that parents will block out the prime-time shows that the most advertising revenue generate.

9. If a show an explicit rating has, parents might block it out and advertisers might shy away.

10. The television industry argues that the V-chip a kind of censorship is since it will indirectly control the kinds of shows produced.

Clauses

A clause is a group of words containing a subject and a verb. Some clauses are **dependent clauses**, meaning that they cannot stand alone as a sentence; other clauses are **independent clauses**, because they can function independently as a sentence on their own. Dependent clauses are often independent clauses that have a **subordinating conjunction** attached to them.

Dependent Clause

Subordinating conjunction	+	Independent clause
Although		we left early
Because		we didn't know
If		we had known
When		we arrived at the movie theater
As		we walked into the dark theater
Since		no one was sitting in the front row
Before		the film was over
Until		the end of the movie

Complex Sentences

Complex sentences contain one independent clause and one or more dependent clauses.

Complex Sentence

Dependent clause	+ Independent clause
Although we left early,	we were still late because of traffic.
Because we didn't know the route,	we took the congested freeway.
If we had known how bad the traffic was,	we would have left earlier.
When we arrived at the movie theater,	the movie had already started.
As we walked into the dark theater,	I tripped over a popcorn box.
Since no one was sitting in the front row,	we took those seats.
Before the film was over,	I remembered I forgot to lock the door.
Until the end of the movie,	we didn't notice that our friends were sitting behind us.

Compound Sentences

Compound sentences contain two independent clauses joined by a coordinating conjunction. They are created by two separate sentences. Examples of coordinating conjunctions are *and, but, yet, or, nor, for,* and *so.* Don't forget to place a comma before the coordinating conjunction.

We were late. We missed the first ten minutes of the film.

We were late, **and** we missed the first ten minutes of the film.

My alarm clock didn't ring this morning. I arrived on time for class.

My alarm clock didn't ring this morning, **yet** I arrived on time for class.

Compound-complex sentences have characteristics of both compound and complex sentences.

Although we left early, we were still late for the film **and** we missed the first ten minutes.

Noun Clauses

Noun clauses are clauses that function as nouns within a sentence. You can use noun clauses to combine two sentences into one, with one sentence functioning as the independent clause and the other as the dependent clause embedded within the main sentence. Consider the following sentences.

    A When I was packing for a camping trip, my mother suggested **B**.

    B I should bring a small first-aid kit.

    C When I was packing for a camping trip, my mother suggested **that** I bring a small first-aid kit.

Sentence C, a sentence created by combining sentences A and B, shows sentence B functioning as a noun clause within sentence A. More specifically, sentence B has become the object of the verb *suggested*. This noun clause is introduced by the subordinating conjunction *that*. The present subjunctive tense (*bring*) shows that it is not a fact (the first-aid kit has not been brought yet), but a suggestion.

Other subordinating conjunctions you might use to introduce a noun clause are *after, as soon as, when, why, how, although, because, whenever, whether,* or *whichever*.

In some cases, a noun clause can function as the subject of the sentence, but usually the dummy subject *it* replaces a potentially lengthy subject. In the sentences below, sentences D and E are combined to produce sentences F and G. In sentence F, sentence E acts as the subject once we add the word *that*.

    D **E** didn't matter to my mother.

    E We were just camping out in our backyard.

    F **That** we were just camping out in our backyard didn't matter to my mother.

However, it is less cumbersome to move sentence E to the end and use the dummy subject *it*, as shown in sentence G.

    G **It** didn't matter to my mother that we were just camping out in our backyard.

Adjective Clauses

Adjective clauses are often used in English to modify a noun; but unlike other modifiers, they come after the noun. They may or may not include a relative pronoun such as *that, which,* or *who*.

The film **he was talking about** was unfamiliar to me.

The book **that had been sitting on the table** has a coffee stain on the cover.

Each sentence above contains two separate ideas and can form two sentences. *The film he was talking about was unfamiliar to me* can produce sentences A and B below.

    A He was talking about a film.

    B The film was unfamiliar to me.

Sentence A contains the adjective clause; sentence B is the main idea. When these sentences are combined, the subject (*the film*) appears only once. The pronoun *that* may or may not appear in this case without changing the meaning of the sentence.

The film **that** he was talking about was unfamiliar to me.

The film he was talking about was unfamiliar to me.

Note that when the relative pronoun is the subject of a verb in the adjective clause, it cannot be omitted.

The movie critics **who** watched the film gave it positive reviews.

Adverb Clauses

An adverb clause is another kind of dependent clause that must be combined with an independent clause. An adverb clause modifies the action of the verb. For example:

Adverb clause   **Independent clause**

When the phone rang, the baby woke up. **(Adverb Clause of Time)**

(The action of the phone, *rang*, woke the baby up.)

Notice that when the adverb clause comes first in the sentence, there must be a comma after the clause.

Adverb clauses also use subordinating conjunctions such as *when, because, that, although, every time, as much as, whenever, even though, while,* or *since*.

Independent clause   **Adverb clause**

He drank some water **because** he was thirsty. **(Adverb Clause of Reason)**

I'm hungry **even though** I just ate. **(Adverb Clause of Contrast or Opposition)**

Exercise 5.4 Compound Sentences

Combine the two sentences to form a compound sentence. Remember a compound sentence is formed by combining two independent clauses using a coordinating conjunction: *and, but, yet, or, nor, for,* and *so.*

> **Example:** Starbucks and Dunkin' Donuts both have interesting histories. They are now rivals in the coffee industry.
>
> **Answer:** *Starbucks and Dunkin' Donuts both have interesting histories, and they are now rivals in the coffee industry.*

1. William Rosenberg opened the first Dunkin' Donuts shop in Quincy, Massachusetts, in 1948. That store still stands today.

   _____

   _____

2. Dunkin' Donuts has always sold donuts. It has sold more coffee than donuts in the last few years.

   _____

   _____

3. Dunkin' Donuts has grown to over 7,000 stores today. The company has plans for more growth.

   _____

   _____

4. The first Starbucks was opened in 1971 in Seattle, Washington. That store is still open today.

   _____

   _____

5. The original plan for Starbucks was to sell coffee beans and coffee-brewing equipment. In 1983, an employee in the company, Howard Schultz, encouraged the owners to sell coffee drinks as well.

   _____

   _____

6. The original owners thought that the main focus should be beans and equipment. They did not take Schultz's advice.

   _____

   _____

7. Schultz started his own coffee shop. He knew that the business would succeed because Americans would buy coffee drinks and not just beans.

_____

_____

8. The original owners sold their chain of Starbucks stores to Schultz in 1987. Schultz immediately increased the number of stores.

_____

_____

9. Today, both Dunkin' Donuts and Starbucks are keen competitors for the coffee market. In many ways, the two shops are quite different.

_____

_____

10. Dunkin' Donuts is said to have a blue-collar customer base. Starbucks is said to have a white-collar customer base.

_____

_____

Exercise 5.5 Complex Sentences

Finish each sentence by creating a dependent clause using the subordinating word provided.

Example: Skateboarding is a risky sport *although* . . .

Answer: Skateboarding is a risky sport although *many kids love feeling the rush.*

1. Snowboarding can be equally risky *if* . . . _____.

2. Still teens especially love the feeling *when* . . . _____.

3. Even high school sports can be dangerous *whenever* . . . _____.

4. For young children, learning to ride a bike is scary *because* . . . _____.

5. Helmets are mandatory in most activities today *because* . . . _____.

6. Each individual state determines *if* . . . _____.

7. Some people in some states think that the sport is no longer fun *now that* . . . _____.

8. In the end, it is the parents who decide *whether* . . . _____.

9. Kids who are underage will have to abide by rules *that* . . . _____.

10. You should enjoy your sport, but you should remember *that* . . . _____.

Exercise 5.6 Noun Clauses

Fill in the blanks with the correct noun clause.

Example: When will you buy a new computer?

Answer: I don't know *when I will buy a new computer.* _____

1. Who invented the Internet?

   We don't really know _____.

2. When did people start buying personal computers?

   I am not really sure _____.

3. To whom was the first e-mail message written?

   I wonder _____.

4. What did the first e-mail message say?

   It would be interesting to find out _____.

5. Where was the first personal computer built?

   We don't know _____.

6. Will computers become less expensive than books in the future?

   It's difficult to determine _____.

7. Did Bill Gates make his money in computers?

   Yes, I believe that _____.

8. Does Bill Gates have more money than Warren Buffet?

   You would have to ask Bill Gates _____.

9. How big is Bill Gates's house?

   I don't know _____.

10. Did Michael Jordan ever make more money than Bill Gates?

    That's a good question. I wonder _____.

Exercise 5.7 Noun Clauses

Revise each of the following sentences by moving the noun clause to the end of the sentence and, if necessary, add the subject *it*.

Example: That airlines limit the amount of carry-on baggage has always frustrated business travelers.

Answer: *It has always frustrated business travelers that airlines limit the amount of carry-on baggage.*

1. That passengers can now only bring one piece of luggage and a hand-held bag into the airplane cabin is a new airline regulation.

   _____

   _____

2. That the piece of luggage meet the new overhead bin size requirements and the hand-held bag fit completely under the seat is now mandatory.

   _____

   _____

3. That travelers couldn't fit everything they needed for a business trip into these small bags was often the case.

   _____

   _____

4. Whichever bags exceeded size restrictions had to be handed over by travelers as checked luggage.

   _____

   _____

5. That the airlines often lost checked baggage irritated many passengers.

   _____

   _____

6. In addition, that checked bags take a long time to arrive at the baggage claim often interferes with busy business travelers' schedules.

   _____

   _____

7. That the airlines have been looking for solutions to this problem is encouraging.

_____

_____

8. That airplanes should increase the amount of space available in overhead bins so that passengers can bring more and larger carry-ons has been suggested by major airlines.

_____

_____

9. That airplanes can achieve departure six to eight minutes faster with the larger bins has been shown by recent studies.

_____

_____

10. Whether flight attendants will be happy about this change is uncertain.

_____

_____

Exercise 5.8 Noun Clauses

Revise each of the following sentences to correct any errors made with noun clauses.

Example: That their computer systems are crashing companies would like to discover the reason.

Answer: *Companies would like to discover the reason that their computer systems are crashing.*

1. Is evident why some companies are becoming concerned about what their employees are doing.

   _____

   _____

2. The amount of e-mail that employees send and receive each day systems administrators can use software to see.

   _____

   _____

3. Is necessary for the company to know that an employee e-mails jokes from a business computer?

   _____

   _____

4. Could be considered a breach of privacy when managers read employees' e-mail.

   _____

   _____

5. One employee said that would sue her company for breach of privacy.

   _____

   _____

6. The systems administrator tells employees that is his job to prevent problems.

   _____

   _____

7. That cause managers to install monitoring software there are many reasons.

   _____

   _____

8. Is true that companies have to buy more bandwidth if their employees send huge amounts of e-mail.

_____

_____

9. Whenever their e-mail is scrutinized but senior executives' e-mail is not lower-level employees are concerned.

_____

_____

10. Is important that managers create an atmosphere that makes employees feel trusted and fairly treated.

_____

_____

Exercise 5.9 Adjective Clauses

Combine each pair of sentences into a single sentence containing an adjective clause.

Example: Teenagers are getting plastic surgery. The number of them is rising.

Answer: *The number of teenagers who are getting plastic surgery is rising.*

1. I spoke to a surgeon. He said that plastic surgery is sometimes a parent's idea rather than a teen's.

   _____

   _____

2. However, more often the teenager is the one. He or she convinces the parent to pay for procedures.

   _____

   _____

3. High school can be a harsh environment. The slightest physical imperfections can provoke torment and teasing.

   _____

   _____

4. Media images of young men and women show impossibly perfect faces and bodies. Teens are frequently exposed to these images.

   _____

   _____

5. Like it or not, we are living in a superficial culture. Attractive people get better treatment than unattractive people.

   _____

   _____

6. Therefore, people are requesting plastic surgery. Their bodies aren't even fully developed.

   _____

   _____

7. One woman was insistent about changing her appearance. She went to a plastic surgeon's office.

   _____

   _____

8. She demanded to have the wrinkles removed. The wrinkles were around her eyes.

_____

_____

9. There were just two problems. The surgeon pointed out these problems to her.

_____

_____

10. The problems were that she was nineteen years old and that she had no wrinkles. The problems prevented her from having the surgery.

_____

_____

Exercise 5.10 Adjective Clauses

Revise the following paragraph to correct the errors in adjective clauses. Some sentences may contain no errors.

> **Example:** For people ~~which~~ *who* are considering plastic surgery, there is a new way to prepare for the procedure.

Nowadays, there are several Internet sites that they show live broadcasts of cosmetic surgery. If people miss the live coverage, they can pull up archival video footage in that patients undergo procedures from liposuction to facelifts. This new trend shows that plastic surgery has gone from something was considered shameful or vain to something is considered normal or even a status symbol. The ten million Americans who had plastic surgery in the 1990s represent every social stratum. Moreover, the majority of Americans whose had plastic surgery came from households that they earned below $60,000. The popularity of the Web casts also demonstrates how much people love to watch live procedures which there is a lot of blood and gore. How do patients feel about being the subject of broadcasts in that their bodies are sliced open? Apparently, just fine; the procedures, are free for patients who model for Web casts, attract hundreds of e-mails per day from candidates.

Exercise 5.11 Adverb Clauses

Fill in the blank with the appropriate subordinating conjunction to complete the adverb clause.

Example: _____*Since*_____ the Hispanic population of the U.S. is growing faster than any other minority group, that is the population candidates are appealing to.

1. Politicians in most states now realize _____ trying to win the Hispanic vote is important.

2. _____ Hispanic Americans come from many different countries and cultures, grouping them together ignores their individual heritage.

3. Cultures from Cuba and Mexico are different _____ cultures of Spain and Puerto Rico are different.

4. _____ not all Irish Americans agree on political issues, there is not a single issue that guarantees all Hispanics' approval.

5. Some issues may capture the interest of the majority of Hispanic Americans _____ demographics present different needs.

6. For instance, _____ many Hispanic Americans desire bilingual education for their children, other Hispanic Americans may not favor bilingual education in schools.

7. _____ the government helps to reduce poverty, it is considered a liberal position.

8. _____ George Bush became president, he broadcast his speech in Spanish to appeal to the Hispanic American voters.

9. His tactic for the broadcast did not meet with full Hispanic approval _____ speaking Spanish is, itself, a hot political issue.

10. _____ these issues exist, listening to and understanding the various cultural differences is crucial to any political candidate.

Exercise 5.12 Adverb Clauses

Revise each of the following sentences to correct the placement of the subordinating conjunction so the sentence makes sense. Remember to add commas when necessary.

Example: Because Andy was late for school, he had a flat tire.

Answer: *Andy was late for school because he had a flat tire.*

1. Andy woke up this morning when he looked out the window.

   _____

   _____

2. He looked at his car in the driveway as he noticed that his tire looked very low.

   _____

   _____

3. Because Andy thought this was strange, he had just gotten new tires the previous week.

   _____

   _____

4. He finished his breakfast as soon as he went out to his car to take a look.

   _____

   _____

5. He came closer to his car as he realized that he had a flat tire.

   _____

   _____

6. He had taken off the flat tire and had put on his spare tire after he drove to his mechanic's shop to get the flat tire replaced.

   _____

   _____

7. He had a warranty on his new tires because the mechanic replaced the tire at no charge.

   _____

   _____

8. The mechanic was taking off the flat tire while he noticed a nail sticking into the rubber.

_____

_____

9. Andy saw the nail when he realized that he must have gotten the flat tire the night before on his way home from school.

_____

_____

10. Because a flat tire was distressing to Andy he had an important exam at school this morning.

_____

_____

Mood and Conditional Sentences

Mood

The term **mood** refers to how the speaker intends a statement to be understood: as a fact (the **indicative** mood), as a command (the **imperative** mood), or as a desire, suggestion, or improbability (the **subjunctive** mood). Most kinds of speaking and writing use the indicative mood. You may also have used the imperative mood when giving instructions or directions, such as "Please shut the door" or "Go down the street and take a left at the light." However, subjunctive sentences occur less frequently and may require more attention on your part to use them properly. Consider the following sentences in the subjunctive mood:

Desire   The customer insisted that her money **be** refunded.

Suggestion   My adviser urged that I **take** my prerequisites before my electives.

Improbability If I **were** an astronaut, I would take my dog with me into space.

The form of the verb determines the mood of a sentence. Present subjunctive is the base form of the verb (the infinitive without *to*). Past subjunctive is the same as the simple past for all verbs except *be*. The past subjunctive of *be* is always *were*. (See Verbs on p. 83 for a review of tenses.)

Conditional Sentences

Conditional sentences are complex sentences that are created by combining a dependent clause (usually beginning with *if*) with an independent clause. (See Clauses on p. 60.) In spoken or written English, conditional sentences express action-and-result relationships: if one thing happens, then another thing results. *If* is usually explicit; *then* is often understood and therefore is usually omitted. In these kinds of sentences, English also distinguishes the degree to which the speaker or writer believes something to be true. In the examples that follow, observe how the indicative and the subjunctive verb forms indicate the speaker's/writer's belief in the likelihood of the statement.

When the speaker/writer believes the **if clause** is likely to happen, the indicative (not the subjunctive) is used. (Remember, the indicative expresses facts, while the subjunctive expresses improbabilities and impossibilities.) The statement below makes a generalization and does not refer to a specific time, so the present tense is used.

If you **get** enough sleep at night, you **function** better during the day.

In the next sentence, the speaker/writer makes a prediction about the future rather than a simple generalization. In this case, the present indicative must be used in the *if* clause and the future indicative in the **then clause** to state the consequences of an action that the speaker/writer believes is likely to happen.

If you **get** enough sleep at night, you **will function** better during the day.

When the speaker/writer doubts that the *if* statement will be acted upon, the past subjunctive is used in the *if* clause and *would* + the base form is used in the *then* clause.

If you **got** enough sleep at night, you **would function** better during the day.

Another alternative to the past subjunctive in this case is *were* + the infinitive, as in the following sentence.

If you **were to get** enough sleep at night, you **would function** better during the day.

When the speaker/writer states an impossibility in the present or in the future, the past subjunctive is used in the *if* clause and *would* + the base form is used in the *then* clause.

If you **slept** with your eyes open, you **would see** how well you sleep.

In the example below, both the *if* statement and the *then* statement have occurred in the past: the chance to get enough sleep in order to function better on that particular day no longer exists.

If you **had gotten** enough sleep at night, you **would have functioned** better during the day.

The speaker/writer is implying that there was too little sleep and, consequently, poor performance. It is possible to express this idea more directly (and therefore a bit less politely) without using a conditional sentence, as in the example below.

You **didn't get** enough sleep last night, so you **didn't function** well.

Exercise 5.13 Conditional Sentences

For each of the following sentences, underline the appropriate verb form from the pair in parentheses.

Example: If an instructor asks that her students (are/<u>be</u>) prepared to discuss a book for class, should they be allowed to watch a "book-to-movie" adaptation prior to the class discussion?

1. Some instructors say that if students (had/will have) access to film versions of the reading assignments, they would neglect to do the reading.

2. An instructor may insist that students (not watch/will not watch) a film version if the class has not yet discussed the reading material.

3. If another instructor (is/were) asked, he might say that watching the film, when done in conjunction with the assigned reading, would enhance the students' learning experience.

4. Such instructors maintain that if students (are/were) to watch only the film version, the quality of their comments would reveal that they had not read the book.

5. Even if students watched a film version of an assigned book, seeing the film (would not take/will not take) the place of reading the book.

6. Also, students may feel that their learning experiences are being limited if they (are/were) not permitted to watch the film version.

7. Some educators are afraid that if a film adaptation of every book (is/were) to exist, students would quit reading books altogether.

8. If students (turn/had turned) to visual media instead of reading their assigned texts, educators feel that the importance of reading will be minimized.

9. A few instructors may even feel that if completion of reading assignments (isn't/wasn't) enforced, film as a medium will replace literary texts.

10. If film (had become/becomes) the preferred medium for the transmission of ideas, will books become obsolete?

Exercise 5.14 Conditional Sentences

In the following paragraphs, fill in the blanks with the appropriate form of the verb in parentheses. You may use modals. More than one answer may be correct.

Example: If people really _____*wanted*_____ (want) to protect their privacy, they would be less willing to give information to stores and Web sites.

If a company (1.) _____ (want) personal information about its customers

badly enough to pay for it, should customers give up their privacy for discounts? A drug-

store chain in my neighborhood has begun to offer a discount card; if customers have this

card, they (2.) _____ (receive) substantial discounts on purchases. The dis-

counts (3.) _____ (appear) when the card is swiped if the customer has pur-

chased selected products. However, customers have to submit personal data such as name,

address, salary, age, and telephone number if they (4.) _____ (want) to receive

the discount card.

When a clerk at the store asked me if I (5.) _____ (want) to sign up

for a discount card, I said no. I thought that if I provided the store with personal

data, they probably (6.) _____ (sell) it to a marketing firm, and then I

(7.) _____ (start) to receive a lot of junk mail and telemarketing calls. The

clerk said that the information would not be sold, but if I (8.) _____ (believe)

that, I wouldn't have refused the card. After all, if the company (9.) _____

(not plan) to sell this information, why are store clerks collecting it?

A friend told me that she (10.) _____ (fill out) a form for the discount card

if she shopped at that store. "They (11.) _____ (use) information about your

favorite products to target you as a customer if you sign up," she said. "Why not let them

do that if you (12.) _____ (be) already a customer of the store?"

If I change my mind about the discount card, I (13.) _____ (think) about

filling out the form with false information. Even if I (14.) _____ (be) homeless, my friend told me, the store would value my business. "All people who shop there should be eligible for the discounts, even if they (15.) _____ (not have) a home address and telephone number," she said. I (16.) _____ (end up) visiting the drugstore as Jane Doe if I decide that my friend is right.

Exercise 5.15 Taking the Next Step with Sentences and Clauses

Write about a wish or a goal that you hope to achieve. This is an ideal way to practice the conditional tense. Consider also using noun clauses and adjective clauses. Refer to the relevant sections of this chapter as you work to help yourself master each concept. Share your wish or your goal with a classmate.

_____

_____

_____

_____

_____

_____

_____

_____

_____

Part 6
Verbs

Verbs are words that show action or states of being. You use them to join the subject to the rest of the sentence. All complete sentences contain at least one verb, which should be in agreement (singular or plural) with the subject of the sentence.

Tenses

A verb tense is the form a verb takes to show when something took place. All verbs except for the verb *to be* have five forms. *To be* has three present-tense forms and two past-tense forms.

Base form	Present (-s form)	Present participle	Past tense	Past participle
work	works	working	worked	worked
file	files	filing	filed	filed
watch	watches	watching	watched	watched
be	am/is/are	being	was/were	been

You can form the **infinitive** by adding *to* to the base form: *to work*. (See Appendix B for a full conjugation of the verb *work*.) The base form and infinitive are not interchangeable, so be sure to avoid substituting one for the other.

You have probably noticed that English has many irregular verbs whose past tense and past participle forms often differ. Consult a dictionary to determine whether or not a verb is irregular.

Simple Tenses

Use the **present tense** to show actions that take place in the present or to show repeated or habitual actions. To form the present tense, use the base form with all subjects except for the third person singular. To form the third person singular, add *-s* to the base form.

He **likes** football.

I **work** on Tuesday evenings.

This machine **operates** efficiently.

Jack and Mary **paint** their house a different color every year.

The **past tense** shows actions that occurred at a particular time in the past. Often a specific time is stated in the sentence. To form the past tense, add *-ed*, *-d*, or *-t* to the base form.

They **worked** for that company a long time ago.

We **vacationed** in Hawaii last October.

The sudden noise **startled** me.

He **slept** well last night.

The **future tense** states an action that will take place in the future. To form the future tense, add *will* to the base form of the verb.

Jose **will work** on that leaky faucet this afternoon.

Her mother **will ask** her to babysit this weekend.

They **will finish** the project by next week.

I'll go by train or bus.

The expression *be going* followed by the infinitive can also be used in a future sense, particularly to state a plan or intent to be carried out in the future.

We **are going to fix** the air conditioning before it gets hot.

Wendy and Dan **are going to visit** Boston in the fall.

I'm going to get my driver's license as soon as I turn sixteen.

She**'s going to look** for a job in the summer to pay for her tuition.

Progressive Tenses

The **progressive** or **continuous tenses**, as they are sometimes called, focus on action in progress or continuing action. You can form them by adding *be* in the appropriate tense to the present participle (*-ing*) form of the main verb.

The **present progressive tense** conveys an action in progress (rather than a completed act). It shows what is happening now. The present progressive tense is formed with *be* in the present tense plus the present participle form.

He **is working** on a solution to that problem.

The dogs **are howling** so loudly that I can't hear myself think.

Dongmei **is sewing** a dress for her daughter.

The **past progressive tense** shows an ongoing action or state in the past that was in progress for a while but is now no longer taking place. Often this tense shows an action in progress interrupted by or taking place at the same time as another action. You can form the past progressive with the past tense of *be* plus the present participle form.

He **was pacing** up and down the room in agitation.

Sharon **was babysitting** when a salesman came to the door.

We **were watching** TV when the electricity went out.

The **future progressive tense** shows action that will begin at a point in the future and will be ongoing for a specified or unspecified period of time. It is formed with *will* + *be* plus the present participle form.

A world-famous soprano **will be singing** at our local opera house.

The boys **will be shooting** baskets after school.

I **will be going** for a walk soon.

Perfect Tenses

While the progressive tenses convey continuous actions or ongoing events, the **perfect tenses** usually convey facts or completed events. You can form present and past perfect tenses by adding the appropriate form of *have* to the past participle form (not the past tense) of the main verb. You can form the future perfect by adding *will have* to the past participle form.

The **present perfect tense** shows an action that occurred or began at a particular point in the past and is still ongoing in the present or has some bearing or effect on the present. It is formed with *have* in the present tense plus the past participle of the main verb.

We **have lived** in Texas for eight years now.

Yasushi and Aiko **have e-mailed** us several times.

Her husband **has rebuilt** their computer's hard drive.

The **past perfect tense** shows an action that occurred in the past before another event in the past. It may be helpful to think of this form as a "super-past" or "double-past" form: it's as far in the past as you can get in English with a single verb form. The past perfect is often used with another verb in the simple past tense (see the underlined verbs in the examples below). It is formed with the past tense of *have* plus the past participle of the main verb.

I **had gone** to college for two years before I <u>chose</u> a major.

Lap **had worked** as a tour guide in Vietnam for three years before he <u>earned</u> enough money to buy a motorbike.

Kim **had managed** to do the dishes, vacuum the floors, and wash the windows before her guests <u>arrived</u>.

The **future perfect tense** shows an action that has begun in the present, is currently ongoing, and will end at a certain time in the future. It is formed by adding *will* + *have* to the past participle form of the main verb for all persons, numbers, and genders.

By the time we get home, we **will have driven** over 2,000 miles in our car in a month.

In May I **will have earned** my degree.

Next summer Tom **will have finished** his book.

The **present perfect progressive tense** indicates an ongoing or continuous action begun in the past and continuing into the present. It is sometimes used with another verb in the simple past tense. You can form the present perfect progressive by using *have* in the appropriate tense plus *been* plus the present participle of the main verb.

I **have been waiting** for this moment for a long time.

Teho and SoYoung **have been looking** for a house for several months.

Juanita **has been taking** piano lessons since she <u>was</u> old enough to sit at the piano bench.

The **past perfect progressive tense** conveys an action that was ongoing for a period of time in the past but is now no longer occurring. Usually this tense shows one action interrupting another action. The past perfect progressive is formed by using *had* + *been* plus the present participle of the main verb.

The ice skater **had been performing** flawlessly when she suddenly fell.

It **had been raining** for days when at last the clouds broke.

Stocks **had been climbing** rapidly when the market fell.

The **future perfect progressive tense** shows an action that has begun in the present and is ongoing into the future, at least up until a time usually named in the sentence. It is used to make projections. You can form the future perfect progressive with *will* + *have* + *been* plus the present participle of the main verb.

> In November, Lucas **will have been working** on his dissertation for two years.
>
> At the end of the marathon, the participants **will have been running** for thirty miles.
>
> Olivia **will have been studying** Japanese for four years at the end of this semester.

Active and Passive Voice

When referring to verbs, the term **voice** indicates whether the subject is acting (**active voice**) or being acted upon (**passive voice**). The tenses in the previous examples are in active voice, because they show the subjects' actions. You should use the passive voice when the acting agent is unknown or not of great importance in the context of the sentence. You can also use it to hide the agency responsible for the action. To form the passive voice, use *be* in the desired tense followed by the past participle form.

> The diamond necklace **was stolen**.
>
> Russian **is written** in the Cyrillic alphabet.
>
> Someone **has eaten** the last piece of pie.

Modals

Modals are auxiliary verbs used most often in making requests and giving instructions. They must be followed by the base form of the verb. The nine most commonly used modals are the pairs *can/could, will/would, shall/should, may/might,* and *must* (which has no pair). In some cases the second modal in the pair refers to the past.

> Elise **can** read a 200-page novel in three hours.
>
> Monica **could** read when she <u>was</u> four years old.

But in most cases, modals usually refer to the present or future. To refer to the past, you must use the modal followed by a perfect auxiliary.

> If you **have** any questions, you **should go** to the instructor.
>
> If you **had** any questions, you **should have gone** to the instructor.

Note that *must* uses *had to* for its past tense.

> We **must** get that contract notarized by 5 P.M. today.
>
> We **had to** get that contract notarized by 5 P.M. yesterday.

When making requests, using the past form of the modal pairs does not change the tense, but instead causes the request to sound more polite because it is less direct. Using different modals can also change the force of a request.

More Direct   **More Polite**

← ──────────────────────────────────── →

Will you get me a drink?
        Can you get me a drink?
                Would you get me a drink?
                        Could you get me a drink?

Here *will* is the most direct; *can* is less direct, *would* is even more polite, and *could* is the mildest form.

Modals can also convey your feelings regarding the certainty of a statement.

Uncertain   **Certain**

←———————————————————————————————————————→

It **might** be time to go by now.

                   It **may** be time to go by now.

                                     It **must** be time to go by now.

Forming Verb Phrases

You can construct verb phrases from a main verb and one or more auxiliary verbs (also called **helping verbs**) such as *be, have, do,* and the modals *can/could, will/would, shall/should, may/might,* and *must.* When forming verb phrases, keep in mind the following rules.

- Verbs must agree with the subject. Sometimes the subject can be challenging to locate when it is separated from the verb by a prepositional phrase or an adjective clause or when the subject is a compound subject.

- Verbs must indicate the time of the action in the sentence by using the past, present, or future tenses. Paying attention to expressions of time in sentences can help you choose the correct tense.

- Except when forming questions, auxiliary verbs require a specific word order: modal + perfect *have* + progressive *be* + passive *be*. (See "Questions" on p. 41 for more information.)

- Only one modal verb should be used in a verb phrase and it must be followed by a base form. (See Modals on p. 86.)

- The base form is never used after any form of *be.*

Exercise 6.1 Simple Present Tense

For each of the following sentences, underline the appropriate verb from the pair in parentheses.

Example: Mobile Bay (<u>plays</u>/playing) host to one of nature's most unusual phenomena.

1. A cry of "Jubilee!" (means/meant) that a multitude of fish and crabs have come ashore in Mobile Bay.

2. No one (knew/knows) for sure what causes a jubilee to happen.

3. Some people believe that a lack of oxygen in the water causes the fish and crabs to (swim/swam) closer to the shore and surface.

4. When a jubilee (occurs/occurred), people grab nets and buckets to easily collect an abundance of sea life.

5. Jubilees always (happened/happen) in the summer, often just before dawn.

6. Local citizens (wished/wish) that they could predict when a jubilee will take place.

7. Some locals (believe/believed) that they can predict a jubilee by watching the weather.

8. Calm water in the bay the day before, a gentle wind blowing from the east, a rising tide, and overcast sky, some believe, (foretell/foretold) a jubilee.

9. Yet jubilees sometimes (took/take) place without all of these conditions present.

10. Regardless of what causes a jubilee, the citizens of the Mobile Bay area (thank/thanks) Mother Nature for the delicious gift.

Exercise 6.2 Simple Past Tense

Write the past tense form of the verb in parentheses in the blank.

      Example: Pirates _____*kidnapped*_____ (kidnap) beautiful women on the high seas
              throughout their long history.

1. The waves _____ (crash) against the side of the schooner as the captain
   reconsidered the validity of his voyage.

2. He _____ (think) that he knew the exact location of his daughter, but now
   he was not certain.

3. Pirates _____ (capture) her three days ago from her home on Serendipity
   Island.

4. The rogues of the pirate crew _____ (dare) her father, Captain Westbrook,
   to come find her.

5. The pirates _____ (leave) a note demanding a lofty ransom for the safe
   return of his daughter, Genevieve.

6. Captain Westbrook _____ (know) that his daughter was tough, but he
   wanted to find her as soon as possible.

7. The first mate of Captain Westbrook's crew _____ (come) to the worried
   father to tell him that his crew supported him 100 percent.

8. When Captain Westbrook and his crew _____ (reach) the shore of Broken
   Bone Cove, he knew his hunch was right.

9. The first mate _____ (find) Genevieve sleeping in an open tent, and she
   was rescued.

10. What a surprise for the pirates the next morning when they _____ (discover)
    that she was missing, and on her pillow was a note from Captain Westbrook daring the
    pirates to come find him.

Exercise 6.3 Present and Past Tenses

For each of the following sentences, underline the appropriate verb from the pair in parentheses.

> **Example:** When I first came to the United States, I (speak/<u>spoke</u>) only a few words of English.

1. After I arrived in this country, I immediately (go/went) to a very large school.

2. I (remember/remembered) that my fourth-grade teachers used to give me books of pictures and alphabet letters.

3. Before long, however, I (become/became) very good at reading.

4. When my family made me return to my native country, I (am/was) so depressed that I didn't leave the house for weeks.

5. They told me, "You can't (lie/laid) around the house. Time to go to school."

6. Three years later, history (repeats/repeated) itself, and my family returned to the United States.

7. I told my American friends that I (am/was) glad to be back.

8. Two years later, I (graduate/graduated) from high school with a 3.87 GPA.

9. The following fall, I (start/started) college.

10. Now I (take/took) courses in business and computer programming to prepare for a career.

Exercise 6.4 Present and Past Tenses

In each of the following sentences, change the italicized verb to the appropriate tense.

began

Example: Several years ago, many states ~~began~~ administering standardized tests in public schools.
                                      ^

1. In 2002, my eighth-grade teacher told us we *have* to take our state's mandated math and reading tests at the end of the school year.

2. My teacher *spends* the whole spring of 2003 drilling us on the practice tests.

3. School officials came to our class and reassured us that we could not pass or *failed* the test. Scores were for school statistics only.

4. Instead, they said that our school and the teachers *are* being tested.

5. The students agreed that nobody *is* fooled by the officials' remarks.

6. My friend Hector said, "The test results *were* going to be sent to our parents."

7. In May of that year, we *sit* in class every day for a week completing the test.

8. I *score* in the fiftieth percentile, so my results were exactly average.

9. Now I think of those results and *remembered* the eighth grade fondly.

10. I still believe that kids *learned* more in school when less time is spent on test preparation.

Exercise 6.5 Present Perfect Tense

Fill in each blank with the present perfect tense of the verb in parentheses.

> **Example:** In recent years, politicians and scientists ___*have proposed*___ (propose) many new technologies to reduce our use of oil.

1. For example, many automakers _____ (begin) to make hybrid cars or cars that run on both gasoline and electricity.

2. Two of the most popular hybrid cars lately _____ (be) the Honda Insight and the Toyota Prius.

3. The Honda Insight, which uses only electricity at low speeds and gasoline at high speeds, was the first hybrid car available. I _____ (drive, not) one, but I have a friend who owns one.

4. The Toyota Prius came along after the Insight and became its main competitor. The Prius uses both electricity and gasoline at various speeds. I _____ (take) the Toyota for a test drive.

5. Over the last three years, I _____ (hear) comments about both vehicles by different owners.

6. The owners of the Honda Insight _____ (tell) me that the acceleration is not great, but the gas mileage is phenomenal.

7. The owners of the Toyota Prius _____ (say) to me that they really do not like the handling of the car at high speeds, but they love the gas mileage.

8. However, I _____ (hear) people joke about the Insight and that they think it looks like a space mobile.

9. Another new technology that many scientists and policy makers _____ (mention) is the hydrogen fuel cell.

10. We _____ (wait) a long time for alternatives to gasoline to be developed. I hope a feasible alternative becomes available soon.

Exercise 6.6 Present Perfect Tense

Fill in the blank with the correct past participle to form the present perfect tense. Every verb in this exercise takes an irregular past participle form.

Example: How to save our environment has _____*become*_____ (became) a concern for everyone from schoolchildren to adults across the globe.

1. Many scientists have _____ (speak) about our need to make changes in our daily lifestyles.

2. Recycling containers have _____ (became) visible in schoolyards across the country.

3. Some countries have _____ (forbid) drivers from driving every day. Motorists with even-numbered license plates drive one day and those with odd numbers drive the next day.

4. To lower the use of gasoline, some states have _____ (draw) up a plan to lower the speed limit on major highways to 55 mph.

5. The environment involves many aspects. It is believed that global warming has _____ (leave) some plants and animals struggling for their existence.

6. Our lifestyles have _____ (lead) to an enormous need for wood for housing and paper supplies. Eliminating trees affects the quality of air that we breathe.

7. In the state of California, visitors cannot enter from another state with plants and fruit because in the past "foreign" plants have _____ (hold) bugs that can harm the environment in their new location.

8. Scientists have _____ (write) documents that show that in just one day, 45 plant and animal species will die and no longer exist on our planet.

9. In many ways, our lives have already _____ (begin) to change.

10. Thankfully, public awareness has _____ (make) all of us think about our part in the cycle of life and a healthier future.

Exercise 6.7 Past Perfect Tense

Fill in the blank with the correct past perfect verb form.

> **Example:** Roberto Clemente, perhaps the most famous professional baseball player from Latin America, died in a tragic airplane accident in 1972. At the time of his death, Clemente _____*had set*_____ (set) many records and _*had accomplished*_ (accomplish) many feats in the game of baseball.

1. Roberto was born in 1932 in San Anton, Puerto Rico. His mother, Luisa, _____ (have) four other children from a previous marriage before giving birth to Roberto.

2. Roberto's father worked in a sugar mill. Sugar _____ (become) the main industry in Puerto Rico by the time Roberto was born.

3. As Roberto grew up in his modest home, he developed a love for baseball. He _____ (become) a star shortstop on a local team before he turned fifteen years old.

4. Roberto's talents in baseball soon became well known to professional scouts. Before he reached the age of nineteen, he _____ (be) drafted by the Brooklyn Dodgers to play on their minor league team, the Montreal Royals.

5. Roberto did not play much, though. The manager for the Royals knew that Roberto already _____ (impress) many people with his great abilities, so he kept him on the bench. He did not want other scouts to notice Roberto.

6. However, Howie Haak, a scout for the Pittsburgh Pirates, _____ (see) Clemente play several years earlier. He was determined to get Clemente to play for the Pirates. In 1954, the Pirates picked Clemente as their first choice in the minor league draft.

7. Clemente played his whole career with the Pittsburgh Pirates. By the end of his last season in 1972, he _____ (help) the Pirates win two world championships and _____ (become) a hero in his native land of Puerto Rico. He was well known for his great abilities in hitting, fielding, and throwing.

8. On December 23, 1972, the city of Managua, Nicaragua, experienced a massive earthquake. Clemente _____ (visit) the city of Managua three weeks before the earthquake. He wanted to help provide emergency aid to the city.

9. Clemente chartered a plane to bring supplies to Managua. However, the plane

_____ (have) many mechanical problems before this time. Clemente

_____ (not be) aware of these past problems before he chartered the plane.

10. The plane, which left Puerto Rico on December 31, 1972, crashed into the ocean right

after it _____ (take off). No one on the plane survived, and Clemente's

body was never found.

11. The nation of Puerto Rico and baseball fans all over the world mourned the tragic loss

of Clemente. The world _____ (lose) a legend.

12. At the time of his death, Clemente _____ (accumulate) 3,000 hits and

_____ (acquire) a lifetime batting average of .317. He also

_____ (win) twelve Gold Glove Awards.

13. On March 20, 1973, the Baseball Writers Association of America voted to put Roberto

Clemente into the Baseball Hall of Fame. Up to this time, no other player from Latin

America _____ (be) given this honor.

Exercise 6.8 Future Perfect Tense

Fill in each blank with the correct future perfect form of the verb in parentheses.

> **Example:** The electronic book has become very popular in recent years. Many people think that by 2015, the electronic book *will have become* (become) as popular as the print book.

1. An electronic book, or an e-book, is a book that is purchased online and downloaded to a computer or an electronic device. Some estimates say that by 2010, every book that will be printed in hard-copy form _____ (publish) in e-book form as well.

2. By the time our children become adults, they probably _____ (read) quite a few e-books.

3. By the time we are retired, we most likely _____ (buy) a few e-books as well.

4. Some observers say that by 2050, perhaps e-books _____ (become) more popular than print books.

5. Some companies are making devices that can store e-books. Some of my friends say that by 2025, every college student _____ (obtain) one of these devices.

6. They say that college students will not go to a bookstore to buy their textbooks in the future. By the time people attend college in 2025, they _____ (get) used to buying their books online.

7. In fact, by 2020, some argue that they _____ (forget) what a bookstore looks like!

8. Other forms of technology may advance along with the e-book. For example, by the time e-books become more popular than printed books, all of our automobiles _____ (be equip) with electronic devices to read text on the dashboard.

9. Of course, many people do not believe e-books will replace printed books. I hope this will not be the case. If this does happen, hopefully I _____ (reach) such an old age that it won't matter if I can read a computer screen or not.

10. By the time bookstores go out of business because of e-books, I _____ (become) too old and too tired to walk to a bookstore anyway!

Exercise 6.9 Perfect Tenses

Fill in the blank with the correct perfect verb tense. Then identify each verb as present perfect, past perfect, or future perfect tense.

> **Example:** Students _have participated_ (participate) in student government for seventy-five years in American high schools and universities. _present perfect_

1. Our university student body president _____ (consider) running for public office upon graduation.

2. Upon graduation, she _____ (spend) four years serving the students of Farris University.

3. Before college, she _____ (serve) in high school student government.

4. By her first day after graduation, Megan _____ (provide) a total of eight years in student government.

5. Her parents _____ (hope) that Megan would attend medical school to become a pediatrician.

6. Megan _____ (try) to persuade her parents to embrace her potential career choice in the area of public service.

7. They consistently remind her that from the time Megan was ten years old, she _____ (dream) of becoming a doctor.

8. Mr. and Mrs. Wilcox _____ (want) Megan to make a difference in the world through practicing medicine.

9. Megan _____ (assure) her parents that no matter what she chooses, she will work diligently to make the world a better place.

10. By the time of commencement, Megan _____ (decide) on a career choice, and she is planning to announce what it is during her address to the student body.

Exercise 6.10 Progressive Tenses

Of the two choices in parentheses, underline the choice that is correct.

Example: The Alford family (<u>are moving</u>/is moving) to Austin, Texas.

1. Dr. Alford (was teaching/has been teaching) as an adjunct professor at the University of Texas during the past three years.

2. Dr. Alford (was receiving/has been receiving) wonderful evaluations from his students this year in particular.

3. The chancellor (were noticing/was noticing) how respected he was, and so the chancellor offered Dr. Alford a permanent teaching position.

4. His family (be hoping/is hoping) that they will enjoy living in Austin for the entire year.

5. They (was visiting/had been visiting) during the years when Dr. Alford taught, and they always enjoyed their visits.

6. Dr. and Mrs. Alford (are hunting/is hunting) for a house in Austin today.

7. They (will looking/will be looking) for a home that is near the university campus.

8. The children (are wishing/is wishing) for a house near the park.

9. No matter where they live, the Alford family (is looking/are looking) forward to Dr. Alford's dream being realized.

10. Now that Dr. Alford has achieved his career goal, Mrs. Alford (is wondering/are wondering) what her next step should be.

Exercise 6.11 Active and Passive Voice

Of the two choices in parentheses, underline the choice that is correct.

Example: The first e-mail system (used/<u>was used</u>) by the Massachusetts Institute of Technology in 1965.

1. Electronic mail, or e-mail, (invented/was invented) by many people.

2. When computers began to be networked together in the late 1960s, a system had to (develop/be developed) to allow users of different computers to communicate with each other.

3. Just as the postal service needs an address on an envelope to send a letter, the computers (needed/were needed) an address to be able to send messages to computer users.

4. Ray Tomlinson (gives/is given) credit by many people for inventing e-mail in 1972.

5. Tomlinson (selected/was selected) the "@" symbol for all e-mail addresses to indicate that a message was to be sent from one computer user to another.

6. By 1974, hundreds of people in the military (were using/were being used) e-mail on a computer network called ARPANET.

7. Larry Roberts then (developed/was developed) a system of placing e-mail messages into folders.

8. By 1976, commercial vendors (began/were begun) to sell e-mail packages and services.

9. While Tomlinson and Roberts developed many advancements that allowed the use of e-mail to grow, neither one (can call/can be called) the inventor of e-mail.

10. As the World Wide Web began to develop, e-mail (made/was made) available to masses of people as a means to communicate by computer.

Exercise 6.12 Active and Passive Voice

Fill in the blank with the correct voice of the verb—either active voice or passive voice.

Example: *The World Is Flat* ____*was written*____ (write) by Thomas Friedman.

1. In the book, Friedman _____ (analyze) the development of globalization throughout the world.

2. The book _____ (release) in 2005, but then expanded editions _____ (publish) in 2006 and again in 2007.

3. In the book, Friedman recalls a trip that he _____ (take) to Bangalore, India. There he realized that globalization _____ (make) the world "flat" because it had leveled the competitive relationships between industrial nations and emerging nations.

4. Friedman identifies ten different developments in the world today that are "flattening" the global economy and _____ (cause) distant companies to work together.

5. For example, outsourcing allows different manufacturing tasks to _____ (subcontract) to other companies overseas.

6. Another example is open sourcing. This practice _____ (allow) people in different countries to collaborate on projects online.

7. Friedman also argues that many regional differences among different groups _____ (eliminate) because of globalization.

8. Friedman notes that workforce training in the United States must _____ (update) so that workers can possess skills needed in the global economy.

9. He also says that young people should _____ (encourage) to study science, engineering, and mathematics.

10. The book _____ (generate) much discussion, as not all people have agreed with its conclusions.

Exercise 6.13 Modals

For each of the following sentences, underline the appropriate modal from the pair in parentheses.

Example: Fifty years ago, most people (cannot/<u>could not</u>) learn to use computers.

1. Today, few Americans (will/would) consider living without the conveniences they take for granted.

2. People in the United States (can/could) perform many daily tasks easily because tools to simplify life are widely available.

3. Financial tasks are one example of chores that (will/would) have been more difficult in the years before home computers.

4. Now, Americans (can/could) use computers to view their accounts and pay their bills.

5. With the right computer software, ordinary people (may/might) do their own taxes rather than hire accountants or try to understand the fine print in tax forms themselves.

6. Software today includes more information about current tax law than most people know, and software of all types (should/would) continue to become more sophisticated.

7. Household chores (can/could) also take more time if Americans did not have appliances made more efficient by technology.

8. What modern kitchen (will/would) be complete without an automatic dishwasher?

9. Washing dishes by hand (would/should) take more human effort than loading a dishwasher, and filling a sink to wash dishes (might/may) even use more water than running the machine.

10. (Would/Will) Americans ever miss doing chores the old-fashioned way?

Exercise 6.14 Modals

Revise each of the following sentences to show the correct use of modals.

Example: Before I enrolled at the university, I thought that getting any kind of degree
would
~~will~~ help me get a job.
^

1. I soon discovered that I must choose a major after two years of coursework.

2. I cannot decide what career field interested me most, so selecting a major was difficult.

3. At the beginning of my third year of coursework, I must make a choice.

4. My adviser told me that I can change my mind later if I decided I wasn't happy with my decision.

5. I decided that I will study engineering.

6. When I took my first engineering course, I discovered that I can't understand some of the math required to complete my homework assignments.

7. I realized that I would have taken more advanced math courses to prepare for my engineering classes.

8. Now I am taking an extra math course to catch up, and I would finish my engineering degree next spring.

9. I can't wait until I start work as an engineer.

10. In the meantime, my professors tell me that I would study diligently to prepare for my career.

Exercise 6.15 Modals

For each of the following sentences, fill in the blank with an appropriate modal and the correct form of the verb given in parentheses. More than one answer may be correct.

> **Example:** People who are considering travel outside their native country
> ___*should learn*___ (learn) about the culture and language of the country they plan to visit.

1. If I had planned the time before my trip more carefully, I _____ (study) the language and culture before traveling.

2. In my first few weeks out of my own country, I _____ (struggle) to communicate in all my interactions with people.

3. I _____ (consider) returning to my native country immediately, but I knew I would regret it later.

4. If I hadn't been so curious about the country I was visiting, I _____ (stay) in my apartment.

5. But, in order to make the most of my time away from home, I knew I _____ (venture) out on my own and face the language barrier.

6. Now, after living here for more than a year, I _____ (enjoy) the culture much more, because I have learned the language well.

7. In fact, I _____ (have) a difficult time readjusting to my native environment if I returned.

8. If I returned home now, I am afraid that I _____ (feel) the same alienation in my native country that I felt when I first arrived in this country.

9. Besides, I _____ (miss) my new friends if I left this country.

10. When my family comes to visit me here, I _____ (prepare) them for the many cultural differences I encountered here over a year ago.

Exercise 6.16 *To be* Verbs

For each of the following sentences, underline the appropriate form of the verb given in parentheses.

    Example: The Benny Goodman Orchestra (<u>was</u>/were) famous for playing big band music.

1. Attending orchestral concerts (is/are) a great source of fun for people of all ages.

2. Matt, Ling, and I (are/am) attending a concert tonight.

3. It (is/be) a big band concert featuring the works of Benny Goodman, complete with dancing.

4. Big band music (were/was) extremely popular in the 1930s and 1940s, packing dance halls across the nation.

5. When big band music played, couples (was/were) filling the dance floor with swing dancing.

6. Matt and Ling (are/am) hoping that a swing dancing contest will be held at the concert tonight.

7. They (was/were) practicing their swing dance moves last night until midnight.

8. They (is/are) leaving soon so that they can claim a seat with a good view of the stage.

9. I (am/are) meeting them at the venue at six o'clock.

10. I wonder if you know how to swing dance, because I (are/am) going to learn and I need a partner.

Exercise 6.17 *To be* Verbs

Fill in the blank with the correct form of the *to be* verb.

Example: At this moment, Laura _____*is*_____ in line waiting to buy tickets.

In the past, Neal (1.) _____ quite a frivolous spender. He and his friends (2.) _____ frequently investing most of their paychecks in dining out and entertainment. His parents cautioned Neal that he (3.) _____ squandering his money and that he needed to (4.) _____ more conscientious about his spending. Neal realized that his parents (5.) _____ right. He worked diligently to develop a budget for himself. This strategy worked, and in fact Neal (6.) _____ now very frugal. He packs a lunch to take with him to work, and he (7.) _____ now a regular at the dollar movie theater. I (8.) _____ impressed with the changes that he has made. Though Neal once (9.) _____ a person who was a free spender, he (10.) _____ now a person with a hefty balance in his savings account.

Exercise 6.18 Verb Phrases

For each of the following sentences, underline the appropriate verb form from the pair in parentheses.

> **Example:** In California, hundreds of millions of dollars (spent/<u>are spent</u>) annually to provide bilingual education to students with limited proficiency in English.

1. Bilingual education programs are (regard/regarded) as a failure by many Americans.

2. Many graduates of these programs have not (learn/learned) good English skills.

3. The United States would (face/facing) a serious problem if citizens expected the government alone to meet every need.

4. Some states (are trying/trying) to eliminate bilingual education classes in their schools.

5. Administrators of bilingual programs have not usually (ask/asked) parents and community groups for input.

6. Parents must (involve/to involve) themselves in bilingual programs.

7. Parents who have time should (volunteer/volunteering) with community organizations to propel bilingual education forward.

8. Many people (believe/are believing) that this kind of activism would enable bilingual education to reach its goal.

9. A student could (achieve/achieves) fluency in English with the help of his or her parents.

10. In order to overcome discrimination, citizens must be (unite/united) to solve the language problem.

Exercise 6.19 Verb Phrases

Each of the following sentences contains a verb phrase error. Revise each sentence.

Example: Many people who ~~are~~ study English as a foreign language focus on learning the grammar of written English.

1. Students of English are often surprise by the differences between written and conversational English.

2. Those students who have study formal written English may find conversational English difficult to understand.

3. Students who have recently came to an English-speaking country may have particular trouble with slang vocabulary and expressions.

4. Conversation classes in English supposed to help students become familiar with spoken English by simulating real-life situational dialogues.

5. Students who have not exposed to spoken English can listen to English radio or TV broadcasts to help them learn English.

6. Just listening to spoken English can useful in learning oral speech patterns and intonation.

7. Many students find that listening to songs with English lyrics can helps them learn new vocabulary and expressions.

8. Some students who do not feeling a need to learn spoken English might prefer to listen to radio broadcasts in their native language rather than broadcasts in English.

9. If such students do not make a great effort to learn conversational English, they may never can understand the spoken language well.

10. Students in English classes who may not have working hard on learning spoken English need to understand that an inability to speak and understand English can limit their opportunities.

Exercise 6.20 Simple, Perfect, and Progressive Verb Phrases

For each sentence in the following paragraphs, underline the appropriate verb phrase from the pair in parentheses.

Example: In the past ten years, bottled water (became/<u>has become</u>) increasingly popular in America.

While I (shopped/was shopping) at a grocery store last week, I (counted/was counting) five different brands of bottled water on the shelves. These days, bottled water (costs/is costing) more than carbonated beverages, but many consumers now (feel/are feeling) that good health is worth the greater price.

Nutrition experts (have observed/have been observing) that Americans (consume/have consumed) too much soda and junk food. Prior to these findings, some parents (noticed/have noticed) that their children were more sluggish and inattentive after they (had eaten/were eating) junk food. In many cases, they (had been snacking/have been snacking) at school.

Now nutrition experts insist that children (need/are needing) breakfast before school so that they (do not stop/have not been stopping) at vending machines for sodas or greasy snacks. Because studies (showed/have shown) that students perform better when they eat nutritious foods, some schools (consider/are considering) a ban on certain junk foods and soda machines.

However, many parents (believe/are believing) that good nutrition should be enforced by parents, not schools. They (resent/are resenting) being told by the school administration what not to put in their children's lunch. Based on recent sales of bottled water, it (appears/is appearing) that consumers (make/are making) better nutritional choices.

Exercise 6.21 Simple, Perfect, and Progressive Verb Phrases

Revise each of the following sentences by correcting errors in verb phrases, using simple, perfect, and progressive verb forms where appropriate.

Example: In 1954, the U.S. Supreme Court ~~has~~ desegregated education, declaring that "separate educational facilities are inherently unequal."

1. Since then, the states often challenged the federal government either by ignoring or refusing to implement the decision or by filing court cases.

2. The case of Central High School in Little Rock, Arkansas, has been one of the most famous examples of a state fighting this federal mandate.

3. When the school has opened in September 1957, the Arkansas National Guard was called out to prevent African Americans from entering the school.

4. President Dwight D. Eisenhower ordered the army into Little Rock to enforce the court order, and African American children finally were entering the school with the protection of federal troops.

5. State-supported resistance to desegregation was not ending with the Little Rock case.

6. However, over the years the courts consistently ruled in favor of desegregation.

7. Racial integration of schools is remaining a concern for the current generation as well.

8. Recent statistics are showing that about 35 percent of African American students go to schools in which 90 percent of the student body is nonwhite.

9. In addition, support for integration declines in the current political climate.

10. Today, the fight for desegregation was largely replaced by the fight for quality education for all students.

Participles

Participles are adjectives that have been created from verbs by adding suffixes (for regular verbs, usually *-ed* and *-ing*).

A **participial adjective** is a participle that describes a noun. You can often use the present active and past active participles as adjectives, particularly to describe feelings or actions. The **present participle** describes the thing or person causing the feeling or action. The **past participle** describes the person having the feeling or experiencing the action.

An **interesting** article was in the newspaper today. (present participle: *interesting*)

All **interested** parties were encouraged to apply for the position. (past participle: *interested*)

The **boring** lecture finally came to an end. (present participle: *boring*)

The **bored** student had fallen asleep in his chair by the time class was dismissed. (past participle: *bored*)

The **cutting** remark brought tears to Kate's eyes. (present participle: *cutting*)

The **cut** padlock proved that someone had accessed the storage unit without permission. (past participle: *cut*)

A **frightening** shadow appeared in the doorway. (present participle: *frightening*)

Hearing a loud peal of thunder, the **frightened** girl ran to her mother. (past participle: *frightened*)

Infinitives and Gerunds

While an infinitive is a verb form and functions as a verb, a gerund only *appears* to be a verb (it looks like a progressive form), when in fact it is actually a noun derived from a verb. Choosing between infinitives and gerunds can present difficulties for non-native speakers. Generally, you should use infinitives when stating intentions, desires, or expectations; you should use gerunds to state facts or events.

Sergey **wants to work** at the local coffee shop. (infinitive: *to work*)

Dr. Brenes **started working** on her new book this summer. (gerund: *working*)

However, you should use a gerund, not an infinitive, following a preposition.

A stethoscope is used **for listening** to heartbeats. (gerund: *listening*)

A stethoscope is used **to listen** to heartbeats. (infinitive: *to listen*)

These cookies were made **for eating**. (gerund: *eating*)

These cookies were made **to eat**. (infinitive: *to eat*)

Exercise 6.22 Participles

In each of the following sentences, underline the participles.

> **Example:** The <u>soaring</u> balloons high above the crowd are a typical sight at parades across the country.

1. The flags of the color guard appeared around the corner, signaling the beginning of the parade.

2. The cheering crowd welcomed the first procession of the Mardi Gras season.

3. Thousands of onlookers packed the sides of the downtown streets in anticipation of catching beads and trinkets.

4. Each parading Mardi Gras organization has a different theme each year for its procession.

5. The theme of this particular parade is "Smiling Faces," and each float features a famous comedian.

6. Carrying torch-lit signs, men dressed as court jesters announce the name of each float.

7. Enormous floats slowly pass by as their riders throw beads and plastic cups to the waving crowd.

8. My favorite float was the Charlie Chaplin float, featuring a gigantic rendition of his famous character, the tramp.

9. Ten marching bands, twelve floats crowded with masked revelers, and an entire cast of horses, clowns, and silly characters combine to form the parade.

10. A parade of a different type immediately follows each Mardi Gras parade; rumbling in unison, the street sweeper trucks prepare for their big moment as the last float passes.

Exercise 6.23 Participles

Write the correct participial form of the verb given in parentheses.

Example: The sun was _____*shining*_____ (shine) and the birds were
_____*chirping*_____ (chirp) in the park during Nancy and Joe's time together.

1. _____ (Carry) the heavy picnic basket, Joe searched with Nancy for a lovely spot in the park to have lunch.

2. Joe's stomach was _____ (growl) as he reached inside the basket and grabbed a sandwich.

3. He consumed the entire sandwich without Nancy's _____ (notice).

4. "This spot is _____ (overflow) with ants," said Nancy. "Let's try on the other side of the park."

5. _____ (Wander) aimlessly, the couple searched from one end of the park to the other.

6. Joe was _____ (eat) the entire time that it took for them to find the perfect location for their picnic.

7. The _____ (roam) couple at last discovered a shady, dry place with no ants.

8. They both decided that it was the perfect _____ (picnic) spot, and they spread out the blanket.

9. Without _____ (look) into the basket, Nancy reached in to get a sandwich but discovered that the basket was empty.

10. She turned to Joe, who was _____ (finish) the last bit of food that was packed for lunch!

Exercise 6.24 Participial Adjectives

For each of the following sentences, underline the appropriate participial adjective from the pair in parentheses.

Example: One of the most (fascinated/<u>fascinating</u>) recent developments in medicine is the use of robots in surgery.

1. Many doctors are (excited/exciting) about the advantages robots have over humans in medicine.

2. Of course, a robot will never be able to calm a nervous patient with a (soothed/soothing) explanation of a medical procedure.

3. A (terrified/terrifying) patient about to undergo surgery might prefer a human doctor.

4. However, robot "surgeons" never become (tired/tiring) when standing for hours during an operation.

5. Of course, an (observed/observing) doctor will control the robot's actions.

6. Surgical robots can correct the movements of a doctor's (shaken/shaking) hands.

7. These robots, equipped with cameras, magnifying lenses, and bright lights, allow doctors an (amazed/amazing) view inside the human body without the need for large incisions.

8. Robotic surgical assistance should decrease the number of (horrified/horrifying) problems that can happen during and after surgery because of human errors.

9. Instead, the robots and their human operators can complete surgery with more (satisfied/satisfying) results.

10. Someday, surgical patients may be (surprised/surprising) to learn that their doctor had mechanical assistance during the operation.

Exercise 6.25 Participial Adjectives

Revise any of the following sentences that do not use participial adjectives correctly. If a sentence does not contain an error, write **C** above it.

> **Example:** The ~~astonishing~~ *astonished* medical students could hardly believe the realism of their new ^ mechanical practice patient.

1. Suffered patients have been used for medical students' practice in teaching hospitals for decades.

2. No matter how interested a student is in medical school lectures, the lectures cannot prepare him or her to perform procedures on patients.

3. Sitting in a packing lecture hall, first- and second-year medical students can only imagine working on a real patient.

4. However, disgusting patients soon tire of having amateurs use them to practice starting IVs, drawing blood, and giving injections.

5. Repeated practice is absolutely necessary for good medical technique, but what patients are willing to let medical students spend hours prodding and poking them?

6. New technologically advanced fiberglass "patients" allow fumbling medical students to practice on them for as long as the students wish.

7. A distressing medical student may choke a mechanical patient repeatedly while trying to put a tube down its throat, and the machine will utter a loud gagging noise.

8. The gagging sound is unnerved, but students' mistakes do not hurt any living human beings.

9. The uncomplained mechanical patients allow students to develop good medical technique before they handle real people.

10. When these teaching techniques become more widespread, hospitalized people all over the United States will be relieving.

Exercise 6.26 Infinitives and Gerunds

For each sentence in the following paragraphs, underline either the infinitive or the gerund given in parentheses.

> **Example:** Anyone who plans (<u>to study</u>/studying) in another country should be aware
> that university systems differ from place to place.

Since a university education in one country may differ from a university experience in another, students studying outside their native country may struggle (to understand/understanding) educational attitudes within foreign institutions. For example, in some countries students are expected (to avoid/avoiding) (to speak/speaking) in class, but in other countries it is expected, if not required. Moreover, instructors in some countries encourage students (to participate/participating) actively by (to solve/solving) problems in groups, (to make/making) presentations, and (to examine/examining) case studies.

Another aspect of the foreign classroom that is often confusing is the teacher-student relationship. In many countries this relationship is a formal one; in other countries it can appear (to be/being) more relaxed. Regardless of the level of formality between teacher and student, students should remember (to meet/meeting) deadlines for assignments and (to treat/treating) the professor with respect. Even if a professor meets with students outside of class (to have/having) coffee with them, this shouldn't make the professor appear (to be/being) any less of an authority figure.

Exercise 6.27 Infinitives and Gerunds

For each of the following sentences, fill in the blank with the appropriate infinitive or gerund formed from the verb given in parentheses.

Example: It is easy to understand foreign students' _____*being*_____ (be) confused about grades in American university classes.

1. Most U.S. professors prefer their students _____ (work) independently, but professors do offer help to students who need it.

2. University policies forbid students _____ (share) answers on a test.

3. However, instructors often encourage their students _____ (collaborate) in teams on projects other than tests and papers.

4. Universities consider _____ (plagiarize) written work as grounds for expulsion.

5. Dishonest students may jeopardize their relationship with other students who resent their _____ (cheat).

6. Instructors expect students _____ (do) the work for a class even if the work will not be graded.

7. Some teachers believe that not grading an assignment enables students _____ (judge) their own work.

8. If students want to improve their grades, professors often support students' _____ (work) with a tutor.

9. But most professors don't appreciate their students' _____ (ask) about grades on a test or paper in the middle of class.

10. Students who want class time to discuss grades risk _____ (anger) their professors.

Exercise 6.28 Infinitives and Gerunds

Revise each sentence to correct any errors in the use of infinitives and gerunds.

Example: Understanding the nature of competition in an American university is
necessary for students succeeding there.
to (inserted before succeeding, with *ing* crossed out)

1. International students who are considering to study in the United States should realize that relationships between students here can be either cooperative or competitive, depending on the class.

2. International students who expect cooperating with classmates may initially feel uncomfortable with the competition in American schools.

3. Of course, they should not hesitate asking their classmates for help.

4. In some courses, however, the instructor might decide calculating students' grades in relation to one another.

5. This method of to grade is called a "curve."

6. When a curve is used, students may be reluctant sharing their lecture notes with others because they don't want to hurt their own grades.

7. Students without high grade-point averages risk not to get into a top graduate program.

8. Employers trying to fill a job opening may also choose looking at a candidate's grade-point average and faculty recommendations.

9. When students under pressure are asked deciding between helping classmates and decreasing competition for a high grade-point average, they often choose the latter.

10. International students sometimes have to get used to function in this competitive system.

Exercise 6.29 Taking the Next Step with Verbs

Describe a favorite sport or hobby you enjoy. Be sure to use as many of the verb forms and vocabulary you learned in this chapter as you can. Refer to the relevant sections of this chapter as you work to help you master each concept. Share your sport or hobby with a classmate.

_____

_____

_____

_____

_____

_____

_____

_____

_____

Part 7
Modifiers

Determiners

Determiners are a class of modifiers—words that describe other words. They include the following common words.

The articles **a/an**, **the**

this, **these**, **that**, **those**

my, **our**, **your**, **his**, **her**, **its**, **their**

whose, **which**, **what**

all, **both**, **each**, **every**, **some**, **any**, **either**, **no**, **neither**, **many**, **more**, **most**, **much**, **(a) few**, **(a) little**, **several**, **enough**

Possessive nouns and noun phrases (**Emily's**, **her uncle's**)

The numerals **one**, **two**, **three**, and so on

Noun phrases containing a singular count noun must begin with a determiner.

the museum

my digital camera

a feather

that brown cow

Noncount and plural count nouns may or may not have determiners, depending on the meaning intended:

Exercise is good for you.	=	Exercise in general is good for you.
This exercise is good for you.	=	This specific exercise is good for you.

When choosing determiners, be sure to remember which determiners go with each type of noun.

this, **that** + **singular count or noncount nouns**

this newspaper, that tea

these, **(a) few**, **many**, **both**, **several** + **plural count nouns**

these eggs, a few students, many examples, both candidates, several packages

(a) little, **much** + **noncount nouns**

a little cream, much trouble

some, **enough** + **noncount or plural count nouns**

some cereal, enough time

a, **an**, **every**, **each** + **singular count nouns**

a stereo, an elephant, every person, each day

Exercise 7.1 Determiners

In the following paragraph, underline the determiners. The first sentence has been done for you.

Historically, Japan has not been <u>a</u> country that encouraged immigration. The current labor shortage, however, may force that country to start allowing immigration. Because of Japan's low birthrate, not enough new workers are entering the workforce. Then, when women do have children, few new mothers stay in the job market. In addition, Japan's population is aging faster than the population of any other developed nation. Soon, four times as many Japanese citizens will be over age sixty-five as will be under that age. For these three reasons, the country will not be able to achieve economic growth or support itself unless it expands its labor pool. What strategy would have a more immediate effect than inviting immigration?

Exercise 7.2 Determiners

For each of the following sentences, underline the appropriate determiner from the pair in parentheses. **X** means "no determiner."

> **Example:** Getting (X/<u>a</u>) good education is the most certain way to get a good job.

1. Many people decide to immigrate to the United States for their (children/children's) education.

2. Immigrant parents must also worry about finding (a/some) job to support their families.

3. There are not (many/much) good opportunities for immigrants who have no education.

4. Often, uneducated immigrants end up getting (X/a) jobs with low pay.

5. They are likely to live in (X/a) poor neighborhood.

6. In the United States, schools get some money for (they/their) budgets from taxes paid in the area.

7. (Many/Much) schools in poor neighborhoods do not have enough money to pay teachers well or to provide good facilities for students.

8. Unfortunately, (X/a) student from a poor neighborhood may have to be exceptionally motivated to get a decent education.

9. (Every/All) children should have an equal opportunity to be educated and find fulfilling work.

10. Perhaps someday (X/this) ideal will become a reality for all of (America/America's) children.

Exercise 7.3 Determiners

Each of the following sentences contains an error in the use of determiners. Revise each sentence by adding, deleting, and changing determiners wherever appropriate.

Example: The average American is afraid to speak in front of ^*a* group.

1. Much businesses today expect executives to be good public speakers.

2. In fact, person who cannot speak well in public is unlikely to be promoted to an executive position.

3. However, 40 percent of all Americans have terrible fear of public speaking.

4. For these people, giving some speech is usually a miserable experience.

5. Experts suggest a little ways to help conquer a fear of public speaking.

6. Taking few deep breaths before a speech gives the speaker extra oxygen and can calm nerves.

7. Some speakers feel more confident when they imagine the audience in they underwear.

8. When speakers remember something that made them laugh recently, funny memory can help them to relax.

9. People who have an extreme problems with public speaking might need professional help.

10. Many organizations can help to conquer a businessperson fear of giving speeches.

Exercise 7.4 Determiners

Underline the appropriate determiner from the pair in parentheses.

Example: Craving (a few/<u>a little</u>) sugar can be a lifetime struggle for most people.

Some people believe that having (1.) (any/a few) sweets in your diet will not harm your

health. Others say that even (2.) (a little/a few) bit of sugar can be harmful. Most people

will admit that not eating (3.) (a little/any) sweets is very hard to do. But there are

(4.) (a few/any) things you can do to maintain a healthy body and satisfy a sugar craving.

One way is to just eat (5.) (a few/a little) bit of a dessert and not the entire portion.

Another thing you can do is avoid (6.) (any/a little) sweet that is extremely high in sugar

and fat, and pick a sweet that has more natural sugars and fewer calories. If you are trying

to lose weight, you should avoid eating (7.) (a little/any) sweets for a short period of time

so your body becomes used to living without sugar. You might be motivated to stick to

your diet if you lose (8.) (a little/a few) pounds. The hardest part about cutting back on

your sugar intake is that after a while (9.) (any/a few) dessert will be tempting. Like

most things, though, moderation is key: don't torture yourself; have (10.) (a little/a few)

bit of dessert.

Exercise 7.5 Determiners

Fill in each blank with the correct determiner. Use **a few**, **a little**, or **any**.

Example: I didn't read _____*any*_____ books over the summer.

1. The bookstore manager placed an order for _____ books on making stained glass and one special book on antiques from ABC Books.

2. The books were expected to arrive in _____ days.

3. When the books didn't arrive by Saturday, the manager knew the books would be arriving _____ late.

4. The manager called the warehouse, but he didn't get _____ answer about why the books were late.

5. _____ bit later, the warehouse supervisor called back to say that a few other bookstores had also not received their orders.

6. He said he didn't know of _____ reason that the books were not delivered.

7. Finally, on Tuesday _____ delivery trucks arrived to drop off the book shipment.

8. Instead of receiving a few books on stained glass, the bookstore didn't receive _____ books on stained glass.

9. Also, instead of receiving one special book on antiques, the bookstore received quite _____ books on antiques.

10. The bookstore manager decided that the next time he ordered books, he would order from _____ store other than ABC Books.

Exercise 7.6 Determiners

Underline the appropriate determiner from the pair in parentheses.

> **Example:** The problem with (much/<u>many</u>) athletes is that their decision to go to college depends on their ability to play a sport.

(1.) (Much/Many) student athletes go on to a university if they receive an athletic scholarship. There are (2.) (many/much) universities that recruit the best athletes from high schools around the country. There is (3.) (many/much) controversy surrounding athletes who get preferential treatment in their academic courses if they are not doing well. (4.) (Much/Some) universities, but not all, have a "no pass, no play" policy. This policy means that if a student does not "pass" an academic course, he cannot "play" in the sports program. This policy not only affects the athlete, but also affects (5.) (much/many) professors. (6.) (Much/Some) professors understand the demands of an athlete's life among practice, training, and games. Others believe that athletes receive too (7.) (some/many) privileges and should be treated just like other students. Even other students say that the athletes get too (8.) (many/much) preferential treatment. In addition, corporate sponsors promote (9.) (much/many) sports and athletes because they recognize the potential income an athlete might bring. There is (10.) (some/much) to be said for how a corporate sponsorship can change an athlete's life.

Exercise 7.7 Determiners

Underline the appropriate determiner from the pair in parentheses.

Example: For (<u>some</u>/any) people, choosing a car is easy. They purchase the same make and model year after year.

1. Automobile manufacturers in the United States face competition from (some/any) of the other big automobile makers around the world.

2. If you look at (some/any) one manufacturer, you will find a variety of vehicles introduced every year.

3. Manufacturers use flashy advertising to try to reach consumers; (any/some) consumers are influenced by the advertising, while others are not.

4. The budget-conscious consumer might say that (some/any) car will do.

5. For (any/some) consumers, the reliability of a vehicle is the most important factor.

6. Others might choose a car based on (some/any) outstanding features such as design, leather interiors, or computerized controls.

7. (Any/Some) manufacturers offer customized cars for their more wealthy customers.

8. With so many choices, it is hard to say which, if (some/any), car is the best.

9. One thing is for certain: (some/any) car must meet certain safety regulations.

10. Here is (any/some) advice: test-drive any car before you buy.

Exercise 7.8 Determiners

Underline the appropriate determiner from the pair in parentheses.

Example: Rare books such as (this/<u>these</u>) were donated to the library by Mrs. Smith after she died.

1. The librarian put (these/this) dictionary in the rare books room.

2. The rare books are stored in (that/those) bookcases with glass doors.

3. The dictionary came from an estate sale on (this/these) side of town.

4. Other rare books are stored in (these/this) room.

5. The oldest books are (this/these) books of maps.

6. They were not published in (this/these) century.

7. Another interesting item in the room is (those/that) wooden globe in the corner.

8. The globe is also from (those/that) older century.

9. All of (these/this) books are so rare that they are treated with very special care.

10. When you surround yourself with these books, you might forget that you live in (these/this) century.

Exercise 7.9 Determiners

Underline the correct determiner from the pair in parentheses.

> **Example:** A neighborhood like (<u>this</u>/these) is a loving combination of parks for children to play, good schools, and helpful neighbors.

1. Every year, more and more people move to (these/this) part of the city.

2. The reason people like to live here is because of all (this/these) beautiful parks.

3. They also like all (that/those) old oak trees.

4. We didn't know (these/this) neighborhood would become so popular.

5. In fact, (that/those) school was built because so many young parents moved here two years ago.

6. All of (this/these) children walk to their school because it is nearby.

7. The school colors and mascots are on (that/those) flags.

8. We were not surprised when (that/those) big blue house was sold in one day.

9. We have thought about moving to (that/those) side of town where it is more rural.

10. One day, we will sell (this/these) house and move to a smaller one.

Exercise 7.10 Determiners

Fill in each blank with the correct determiner, using **this** or **these**.

> **Example:** It was his job to take good care of the fine wood _____*these*_____ pieces of furniture were made of.

1. _____ store sells fine furniture made from real wood.

2. First, the sales associate showed us _____ dressers and beds, which are made from oak.

3. I am more interested in _____ bed, which is made from cherry.

4. _____ dresser matches the bed and bedside tables.

5. The most beautiful bedroom sets are in _____ rooms in the rear of the building.

6. _____ sets also cost twice as much as the other sets.

7. The other thing that I am looking at is _____ living room set.

8. I like _____ sofa because it is made out of leather.

9. I also like it because I found _____ pillows to coordinate with it.

10. _____ might be the last furniture store I will have to look in.

Adjectives

Adjectives are a type of modifier that modify nouns—they number, limit, describe, or otherwise specify what kind of noun you are referring to. They answer the questions *Which?* and *What kind of?*

The **red** balloon

An **overstuffed** armchair

The **large** pizza

This **difficult algebra** problem

In English, adjectives usually precede the noun they describe. Adjectives that are separated from the noun they describe by a linking verb or another verb that functions similarly are **predicate adjectives**.

That dress is **lovely**.

Those eggs smell **rotten**.

Those decorations seem **ostentatious**.

The fox was **quick**.

Many adjectives have comparative and superlative forms as well.

Adjective	Comparative	Superlative
bad	worse	worst
big	bigger	biggest
far	farther	farthest
good	better	best
happy	happier	happiest
sad	sadder	saddest
smart	smarter	smartest

Correct modifier placement can present a challenge for non-native speakers of English. Consider the sequence of modifiers in the sentence below.

That tired, hungry, sad-looking big old brown English hunting dog with the spot on his back looks like he could use a good home.

Here are some general guidelines to keep in mind when using more than one modifier for a noun. You might think it would be impossible to figure out how to choose the correct word order in the sentence above, but a few basic guidelines can help.

1. Determiners go at the very beginning of the phrase.

    That dog

    All or *both* precedes any other determiners (<u>both</u> those dogs); numbers follow any other determiners (those <u>two</u> dogs).

2. Phrases or clauses follow the noun.

    That dog **with the spot on his back**

3. Noun modifiers go right before the noun they modify.

    That **hunting** dog with the spot on his back

4. Any other adjectives go between determiners and noun modifiers.

    That **old** hunting dog with the spot on his back

In cases of two or more adjectives (not including the determiners and noun modifiers), the order is variable, but the following guidelines may be helpful.

1. Subjective adjectives (those that express the speaker's opinions and attitudes) come earlier than objective adjectives (those that express facts or descriptions).

    That **sad-looking** old hunting dog with the spot on his back

2. Adjectives denoting size generally come earlier in the phrase.

    That sad-looking **big** old hunting dog with the spot on his back

3. Adjectives denoting color usually come later.

    That sad-looking big old **brown** hunting dog with the spot on his back

4. Adjectives derived from proper nouns usually come in the middle.

    That sad-looking big old brown **English** hunting dog with the spot on his back

5. Other objective adjectives come in the middle. If the phrase includes more than one adjective for which no particular order exists, you should separate the adjectives with commas.

    That **tired, hungry, sad-looking** big old brown English hunting dog with the spot on his back

While the cumbersome phrase above helps to demonstrate the preferred order for modifiers, it is rare in English. These kinds of wordy constructions are difficult to understand; you should avoid them in your own writing.

Adverbs

Adverbs are a type of modifier that modify verbs, adjectives, other adverbs, or entire clauses. They answer the question *How? Why? When? Where?* or *To what degree?* You can form many adverbs from adjectives by adding -*ly* to the end of the adjective.

Adjective	Adverb
quick	quickly
thoughtless	thoughtlessly
great	greatly
fashionable	fashionably
reasonable	reasonably
strident	stridently
bright	brightly
poor	poorly

However, not all adverbs end in -*ly*, and some adjectives end in -*ly* (*friendly, lovely*). Some common adverbs not ending in -*ly* include *more, most, always, never, not, very, too,* and *much*. Also note that the adverb form of the adjective *good* is *well*, not *goodly*.

Some adverbs modify entire clauses and help to connect the meaning between that clause and the preceding one. Examples include *also, consequently, furthermore, however, likewise, therefore,* and *thus*.

It rained all day yesterday; **consequently**, the picnic was cancelled.

Exercise 7.11 Adjectives

Underline the adjective, and draw an arrow from the adjective to the word that it modifies.

Example: For the <u>excited</u> student, playing in the last game was unbelievable.

1. The tattered jersey hangs from the rafters of the gymnasium.

2. A faded number eight and the name "McCormick" are on the back of it.

3. On the front of the jersey is our school mascot, a dragon.

4. The legend of the jersey is told to all students at the beginning of the year.

5. Years ago, the Dragons were losing a basketball game.

6. It was the final game of the season, and Rod McCormick had never played.

7. Rod was the shortest member of the team.

8. When a star player was injured, the coach put Rod in the game.

9. Rod managed to land an unbelievable shot at the buzzer, winning the game.

10. The next day, the coach hung the jersey from the rafters to remind everyone of the terrific game.

Exercise 7.12 Adjectives

Underline each adjective, and draw an arrow to the word that it modifies. There may be more than one adjective in each sentence.

Example: For most students, writing a <u>final</u> draft is a terrible <u>homework</u> assignment.

1. The overstuffed backpack dangled from a hook by the door of the library.

2. Ellen glanced guiltily at the backpack over the top of a fashion magazine.

3. "Ellen, you'd better get started," said Amy. "The research paper is due on Friday."

4. Shooting Amy a dirty look, Ellen retrieved the backpack.

5. She unzipped the flap so that she could search for her rough draft.

6. The backpack was an unruly mess, filled with books, paper, pens, and an old sandwich.

7. Finally, Ellen found the crumpled draft at the bottom of the backpack.

8. Smoothing the paper out on the table, Ellen realized that Friday was only two days away.

9. Working diligently, she was able to finish the paper, but it was not her best work.

10. When Friday arrived, Ellen turned in the paper knowing that next time, she would not procrastinate.

Exercise 7.13 Adjectives

Revise each of the following sentences to correct any errors in the arrangement of adjectives.

        Example: Attention deficit disorder, or A.D.D., results from a ~~problem chemical~~ *chemical problem* in the brain.

1. Most people with attention deficit disorder display behavioral obvious symptoms such as hyperactivity, disorganization, impulsiveness, and an inability to manage time effectively.

2. These all symptoms affect performance in certain jobs.

3. A.D.D. was once thought to exist only in troublesome a few children, but now experts believe that adults can also suffer from it.

4. Nowadays, new research and openness about the condition help prevent job potential discrimination.

5. Most adults would have trouble remaining completely focused on a thirty-minute boring slide presentation.

6. For an adult with A.D.D., such a task is a cognitive huge burden.

7. Modifications simple in the work routine can help A.D.D. sufferers to be more effective in their job.

8. Organizing paperwork by color and size clears up kinds of some confusion for A.D.D. sufferers.

9. For example, a green large folder might contain invoices, and a small blue folder could hold receipts.

10. If it is not possible for them to change office daily confusing routines, A.D.D. sufferers should consider changing careers.

Exercise 7.14 Adjectives

Read the passage below, and use adjectives from the word list to complete the sentences. The first blank has been filled in for you.

Word List

black   vegetable   faded   neglected   young   cheerful   neat   early   beautiful

The _____*black*_____ crow called loudly from the shoulder of the _____

scarecrow. The _____ garden had not been tended in years. Vegetables no

longer grew in _____ rows, because weeds and briars had taken their places.

In _____ autumn, the house was put up for sale. One day, a car pulled into

the driveway, and a _____ couple got out. They immediately loved the house

and its garden. "This is perfect!" said the man to his _____ wife, and she

agreed. They bought the house and began to tend the _____ garden at once.

By summertime, the house was once again lovely, and vegetables were again growing in

the _____ garden.

Exercise 7.15 Adjectives

Read the passage below, and use adjectives from the word list to complete the sentences. The first blank has been filled in for you.

Word List

thrilling interesting several frightening hard
layered next brave early additional

The origin of the roller coaster is an ___*interesting*___ one. _____ roller

coasters, in fact, did not roll at all. They were slides made from _____ wood

and then covered with _____ sheets of ice. _____ riders would

climb stairs leading up to the back of the slides. Once at the top, the passengers would

rocket down the _____ 50-degree drop and then climb an _____

set of stairs leading to the _____ slide. These _____ slides were a

favorite of Catherine the Great, and legend has it that she had _____ slides

constructed on her estate to entertain guests.

Exercise 7.16 Adverbs

Underline the adverb, and draw an arrow to the word that it modifies.

Example: Robert's grandmother waited <u>anxiously</u> for his arrival.

1. Robert slowly turned the doorknob.

2. The door creaked eerily as Robert peered into the parlor.

3. "Grandma," called Robert loudly, "it's Tuesday—are you ready to go?"

4. Mrs. Stadler finally answered, "Yes, Bobby, I'm packing my shoes now."

5. By 1 P.M., Robert and his grandma were walking briskly to the studio.

6. They regularly spent Tuesday afternoons together.

7. Tuesdays were affectionately known as "dancing days."

8. Grandma thoroughly enjoyed dancing with Robert because it reminded her of dancing with his grandfather.

9. Grandpa Ken had died suddenly last year.

10. Robert especially enjoyed spending time with his grandma and filling in for Grandpa Ken.

Exercise 7.17 Adverbs

Underline the adverb in each sentence, and draw an arrow to the word that it modifies.

Example: The audience could not hear the <u>softly</u> spoken words.

1. Leigh quickly put on her hiking boots and grabbed her duffle bag.

2. Her mom had been waiting patiently for her in the van.

3. "Here's my archaeologist," Mrs. White said proudly as Leigh climbed into the passenger seat.

4. The van made its way speedily across town to the Museum of Natural Science.

5. When Leigh and her mom arrived at the museum, the curator promptly met them at the back door.

6. "Do you have it with you?" the curator asked excitedly.

7. Leigh knowingly patted the duffle bag and nodded yes.

8. The curator led them to a brightly lit room filled with spectators, and he introduced Leigh to the crowd.

9. He said, "My fellow archaeologists, you have all heard of the rare specimen of prehistoric bone discovered recently by Leigh White. She has come to show us her find."

10. The crowd applauded wildly as Leigh lifted the bone for all to see.

Exercise 7.18 Adverbs

Fill in the blanks with an appropriate adverb from the word list. The first blank has been filled in for you.

Word List

fortunately graciously extremely calmly today
especially nervously fast supposedly recently

Gus University is _____*extremely*_____ proud of its men's track team, _____

the star of the team, Andre. Andre runs very _____ . In fact, he

_____ set a new record at Gus U for the 50-yard dash. _____ he is

competing in the state meet. _____, Olympic scouts are coming to watch him

run. Coach Vasquez will be looking around _____, trying to detect the scouts.

_____, Andre is more focused than his coach. _____, he will

stretch his legs, arms, and body in preparation for his main event, the 50-yard dash. If

Andre wins, he will _____ accept the handshakes of Coach Vasquez and me,

the incognito Olympic scout.

Exercise 7.19 Adverbs

Read the passage below. Use adverbs from the word list to complete the sentences. The first blank has been filled in for you.

Word List

actively   anxiously   eagerly   traditionally   quickly   consistently   recently   fiercely

Traditionally , in this school district, Field Day is a competition among local high schools. Every year, students _____ await it. Our coaches talked about team spirit and sportsmanship, but even so the events are _____ competitive. They include track and field events as well as a tug of war. The events move _____ . Competitors _____ wait for their scores. Murray High School has _____ won Field Day, so of course everyone wants to beat them. But this year might be their year to lose. A new event has _____ been added: a poster contest. It means that even nonathletic students can _____ participate in Field Day. The winning poster will be awarded 100 points. Who knows, maybe this year Murray High School can be stopped.

Exercise 7.20 Taking the Next Step with Modifiers

Describe a favorite thing that involves movement and color such as the action in a video game, the design of a car, or the clothing in your favorite music video. This exercise will allow you to practice the use of modifiers, adjectives, and adverbs. Share your favorite thing with a classmate.

_____

_____

_____

_____

_____

_____

_____

_____

_____

Part 8
Prepositions

Prepositions are words that show the relationship between other words. Notice how the meaning of the first sentence below changes when the prepositions are rearranged.

Dave went **from** the university **to** work **with** them.

Dave went **to** the university **with** work **from** them.

Prepositions are followed by a noun or pronoun to form a **prepositional phrase**.

to the university

between them

with my friend

from a big city

for me

When the preposition *to* is followed by a verb in its base form, the two words form the infinitive verb form (*to work*).

Using English prepositions correctly can be especially difficult for ESL writers because there is no one-to-one correspondence in prepositional usage between languages, and usage is sometimes idiomatic. Generally, the use of different prepositions will change the meaning. But in a few cases, you can use different prepositions to express the same thought.

The discussion was **about** the use of the Internet.

The discussion was **on** the use of the Internet.

The discussion was **over** the use of the Internet.

Using *At, In, On*

Using the prepositions *at*, *in*, and *on* correctly can be particularly challenging. Here are some guidelines and examples to help you in using these three prepositions.

Expressions of Time

Preposition	Used to express	Examples
At	specific times	*at midnight,* *at 5:26 P.M.* *at eleven o'clock* *at six*
In	general times or periods of time	*in February* *in 1972* *in the afternoon* *in the meantime* *in these years*

On	specific days and dates	*on Saturday* *on June 23* *on Valentine's Day* *on my birthday*

Expressions of Place

Preposition	Used to express	Examples
At	presence at a specific place or event, or participation in some event	*at the local library* *at a movie theater* *at the tennis match* *at the doctor's office*
In	location inside an enclosed area or an area with specific boundaries	*in the yard* *in my car* *in a bookstore* *in the pool* *in a box* *in an envelope* *in a tree*
On	one object supported by another object with some surface of both objects touching each other	*on that table* *on the road* *on her finger* *on your face* *on the roof* *on a branch*

Below are more examples to help you compare the different uses of *at, in,* and *on.*

At	In	On
at work	in the office	on the job
at the stadium	in the bleachers	on the football field
at the game	in the crowd	on the court
at the zoo	in the aquarium	on the iceberg
at 2:00 P.M.	in April	on Tuesday
at nine o'clock	in October	on July 19th
at midnight	in 1968	on September 13, 2007
at night	in the bed	on a mattress

Exercise 8.1 Prepositions

For each of the following sentences, underline the appropriate preposition from the pair in parentheses. **X** means "no preposition."

> **Example:** Most (<u>X</u>/of) teenagers in the United States work part-time jobs during the school year.

1. Teenagers want to show (X/to) people that they can stand on their own two feet.

2. Because they crave independence, teenagers don't want their families taking care (to/of) them financially.

3. Many adults don't agree (to/with) this idea; they believe that working diminishes precious study time.

4. Not only can working interfere (in/with) schoolwork, but it can also negatively affect teenagers' health.

5. When I was (in/at) high school, my best friend, an excellent student, took a part-time job.

6. She thought she could handle both work and school, but (in/on) fact, she did not have enough time to do her homework.

7. Her grade-point average fell (on/from) 3.95 (to/on) 2.40.

8. Her parents finally objected (to/on) the amount of time she spent at work.

9. The choices teenagers make (in/at) these years will affect the rest of their lives.

10. Teenagers are sometimes confused (on/about) their priorities: are they first and foremost students or workers?

Exercise 8.2 Prepositions

Revise each of the following sentences so that prepositions are used correctly.

Example: Some people argue that work has a positive influence ~~in~~ ^{on} teenagers.

1. Some parents don't make any effort to understand to teenagers.

2. At such situations, the workplace can provide a place for teens to interact with adult role models.

3. At work, teenagers can learn to form relationships between other people.

4. While they are in high school, students spend a lot of time to their friends or in class.

5. Work, in the other hand, often requires teenagers to cooperate with people they may not know or like very well.

6. Working also gives students something to do at the hours after school.

7. Teenagers with nothing to do after school are more likely to get at trouble.

8. A part-time job can allow teens to pay leisure activities that they would otherwise be unable to afford.

9. Having a little money to spend in things they want or need makes teenagers feel more independent.

10. A teenager's ability to succeed both as a student and as a worker depends largely in his or her sense of responsibility.

Exercise 8.3 Prepositions

Underline the correct preposition to complete each sentence in the paragraph.

Example: Vince hit the baseball (down/<u>through</u>) the windowpane.

Frank Stoeber is responsible (for/by) one of the greatest roadside attractions (below/in) the state of Kansas. A farmer (except/by) trade, Frank would save pieces of string by rolling them (into/past) a ball. The more string that Frank would add, the larger the ball would grow. Instead of using the ball of string (for/over) other projects, Frank continued to add (with/to) it. When Frank donated the ball of string to the town (of/through) Cawker City, it was enormous. (Over/Across) one and a half million feet of string was rolled (toward/within) a ball that was eleven feet wide. It was the largest ball of string in Kansas. To ward (upon/off) any potential record breakers, Cawker City holds an annual Twine-A-Thon so that the famous ball of string started by Frank Stoeber can continue to grow.

Exercise 8.4 Prepositions

Fill in each blank with the correct preposition.

Example: Meditation and yoga come _____*from*_____ India.

1. Many people begin yoga looking _____ relaxation.

2. Breathing exercises are about relaxation, too. When you are worried _____ something, it is common to tell yourself to "take a deep breath."

3. Religious prayer is also a form _____ relaxation and meditation.

4. Interestingly, yoga is about prayer as well. It is a prayer _____ a universal god.

5. As you meditate, you are taught to listen _____ your breathing.

6. Some yoga followers concentrate _____ a special word that is repeated over and over again to keep their mind focused _____ the meditation and not on their problems.

7. Hatha yoga is the most common yoga practiced _____ America.

8. Its main premise is an interest _____ the physical forms of health.

9. Perhaps you have heard _____ the word *Zen*, which originated in the practice of yoga. Zen is the awakening of knowledge and wisdom.

10. Next time you are nervous _____ a test, close your eyes, take a deep breath, and think Zen.

Idiomatic Verbs

Some verbs require a specific preposition or prepositions and are idiomatic; these verbs are also called **two-word** or **phrasal verbs**. Examine the following sentences.

> The customer forgot to pay and **walked <u>out the door</u>**.

> As soon as the sun was up, the cowboy **set <u>out</u>**.

The first sentence is what you would expect from an intransitive verb followed by a prepositional phrase. Given the definition and general usage of the words *walk* and *out*, their use here and the meaning that they convey aren't surprising. But notice that in the second sentence the preposition does not introduce a prepositional phrase, nor can it be separated from the verb and retain its meaning in this context: as soon as the sun was up, the cowboy left for some unspecified destination. Here the preposition functions as an **adverbial particle**.

While you generally cannot separate intransitive phrasal verbs from their adverbial particles, some transitive phrasal verbs with direct objects can be separated from their particles by the object. The following examples show two ways to express the same idea using a transitive phrasal verb with a direct object.

> Would you **take down** her phone number?

> Would you **take** her phone number **down**?

When a pronoun is the direct object of a transitive phrasal verb that can be separated from its particle, it must separate the verb from its particle.

> I'll get a pencil and **take** it **down**.

Not all idiomatic verbs are phrasal verbs, however. **Prepositional verbs** also consist of a verb and a preposition that cannot be separated, but (unlike the adverbial particle in a phrasal verb) the preposition appears to introduce a prepositional phrase. See the sentence below.

> My son **takes after** his father.

Here the words *takes after* cannot be separated from each other and still retain their contextual meaning, but *after* seems to introduce a prepositional phrase (*after his father*). Yet the phrase *after his father* means something different in this context than you might expect: the writer is saying that the son resembles his father in some way, either in physical appearance or in behavior. This class of idiomatic verbs also includes those verbs whose meaning is predictable but whose accompanying preposition is less predictable (*approve of*, *listen to*).

Some idiomatic verbs consist of three words. These **phrasal-prepositional verbs** combine **verb** + **adverbial particle** + **prepositional sequence** to create sentences such as the ones below.

> I won't **put up <u>with</u>** <u>his tardiness</u> any longer.

> He won't **get away <u>with</u>** that.

> We **look forward <u>to</u>** <u>seeing you</u> at the family reunion.

Because of the unpredictability of these verbs (in terms of both the preposition the verb requires and the altered meaning that results from their combination), you must learn them on a case-by-case basis. It is best to memorize and practice them as you encounter them in context.

Use the list of commonly used idiomatic verbs in Appendix C, p. 164, to help you complete the following exercises.

Exercise 8.5 Idiomatic Verbs

For each of the following sentences, underline the appropriate word(s) from the pair in parentheses.

> **Example:** When I think (back to/with) my first day of college, I remember that it did not go very well.

1. It started when I woke (up/on) much later than I should have.

2. I took (up/off) for my first class quickly, without even combing my hair.

3. The class was in a building far from my apartment, so I wanted to figure (up/out) a shortcut across the campus.

4. I was about (with/to) cross a lawn on the east side of the campus when I saw the sign that said, "Do not walk on the grass."

5. I didn't want to make anyone angry, but I also wanted to save time, so I ended (by/up) walking across the lawn in spite of the sign's warning.

6. I was nervous about trespassing, but I also hoped that I would get away (with/by) it.

7. When I reached the other side of the lawn, I ran (to/into) a security guard coming down the footpath.

8. I started to sweat but decided that I had to put (up with/down with) whatever reprimand he gave me and just hoped that he would not make me later for class.

9. It turned (out/on) that he had not seen me at all.

10. I arrived at class 15 minutes late and immediately began to take (down/up) everything the instructor said.

Exercise 8.6 Idiomatic Verbs

Underline the appropriate word to complete the two-word verb from the pair in parentheses.

> **Example:** During the past ten years, casual dress has caught (<u>on</u>/up) in corporate America.

1. At first, many companies laid (in/out) guidelines for casual dress on Fridays only.

2. Most companies said that employees had to dress (up/out) on Fridays only if they were meeting clients.

3. There were a few problems, though; for example, what if you ran (into/on) a client on casual Friday unexpectedly?

4. Also, for men, the guidelines often meant simply putting (on/off) khakis and a shirt without a tie.

5. However, for women, it was more difficult to figure (on/out) what was casual but not too casual.

6. Nevertheless, companies tried (on/out) casual Fridays first, and now they are making the whole week casual.

7. Employees will soon wake (up/out) to find that they have a whole closet of useless formal clothes.

8. Will Brooks Brothers close (up/down)?

9. Then employees who are building a new wardrobe will have to start (on/over).

10. So, who gets something (out/off) of the change to casual dress? Casual clothing companies, of course.

Exercise 8.7 Idiomatic Verbs

Each of the following sentences contains an error in the use of idiomatic verbs. Rewrite each sentence.

> **Example:** I used to get ~~across~~ with the smoking crowd.
>   *along*

1. My idea was that kids who smoked cigarettes turned on to be the coolest kids in school.

2. They came off with unusual things to say and they wore cool clothes.

3. I admired them so much that I would go up with whatever they said we should think or do.

4. One day I put up my coolest clothes and decided to try a cigarette, too.

5. I looked down to being more like them.

6. But when I tried it, the cigarette tasted so disgusting that I wanted to throw on.

7. I started to look at those kids in a new way, and I no longer wanted to take up them.

8. They did not seem to notice that I did not want to hang up with them anymore.

9. I realized that I had put off with their silly ideas for a long time.

10. From that day on, I decided to stick on friends who did not try so hard to be cool.

Exercise 8.8 Taking the Next Step with Prepositions

World issues are affecting all of us. Gasoline, food prices, vegetation, water, and global warming are topics on everyone's mind. Now imagine that it is the year 2050. What do you think the ten biggest challenges will be? Will those challenges create a world for the better or worse? Consider your practice with prepositions as you let your mind wander into the future. Share this assignment with a partner.

_____

_____

_____

_____

_____

_____

_____

_____

Appendix A
Glossary

abstract usage Abstract usage refers to the use of prepositions in a nonconcrete, nonphysical sense. In the sentence *The book is on the table*, the preposition *on* is used to show the physical location of the book. Now consider the sentence *The book is on Dostoevsky*. We know that the book is not literally sitting on the author Dostoevsky, but rather that the book discusses Dostoevsky. In this sentence, the preposition *on* is used in an abstract (nonphysical) sense to indicate the subject of the book.

adjective An adjective is a word that modifies a noun or a noun phrase. Adjectives number, limit, describe, or otherwise specify the kind of noun. *I found five small stainless steel flathead screws lying in the bottom of my desk drawer.*

adjective clause An adjective clause modifies a noun, but unlike other modifiers, an adjective clause comes after the noun it modifies. It may or may not use a relative pronoun such as *that*, *which*, or *who*. *The person who stood behind me at the drugstore had a cold.*

adverb An adverb is a word that modifies a verb, an adjective, another adverb, or a clause. Many adverbs are formed by adding *-ly* to the end of an adjective. *He quickly ran out the door to catch the bus.*

adverbial particle An adverbial particle is a word that looks like a preposition but functions as an adverb when used in conjunction with the appropriate verb. Together the verb and its accompanying adverbial particle become a type of idiomatic verb called a phrasal verb. *She got over her illness quickly.* See Part 8, Prepositions, on p. 145, for more examples of phrasal verbs and their particles.

article The articles *a/an* and *the* (also called article adjectives) belong to a class of modifiers called determiners. You should use the indefinite article *a/an* when you do not expect the reader to know the identity of the noun being modified. (*An* is a variant of *a*. It is used directly before a word beginning with a vowel sound.) You should use the definite article *the* when you do expect the reader to know the noun's identity or when you are about to reveal it. *A bird flew across the sky.* The identity of the bird is unknown—it has just been introduced to the reader—so the indefinite article is used. There is only one sky, so the definite article is used.

auxiliary verb Also called helping verbs, auxiliary verbs combine with other verbs (usually *be*, *do*, and *have*) to indicate tense, voice, mood, and type of action. *He will have been waiting at the airport for three hours by the time her plane finally arrives.*

base form The base form is the simplest form of verb, with no grammatical endings. *Go.*

clause A clause is a group of words containing a subject and a verb. Some clauses are dependent clauses, meaning that they cannot stand alone as a sentence; other clauses are independent clauses because they can function independently as a sentence.

comparative form The comparative form is an adjective or adverb used in making comparisons between two things. Comparative adjectives usually end in *-er*. Comparative adverbs are often formed from adjectives by adding the modifier *more* before the adjective. *She is taller than her husband. You should dress more appropriately the next time you go out in the rain.*

complex-compound sentence A sentence that is both complex and compound is a complex-compound sentence. *Since my father was tired of driving, he stopped at a motel and we spent the night there in Tucumcari.*

complex sentence In a complex sentence, a dependent clause is joined to an independent clause. *Since my father was tired of driving, he stopped at a motel.*

compound sentence In a compound sentence, two independent clauses are joined by a coordinating conjunction. You can create a compound sentence from two separate sentences. *My father stopped at a motel, and we spent the night there in Tucumcari.*

conjunction A conjunction is a word that joins other words, phrases, clauses, or sentences. Types of conjunctions include coordinating conjunctions, correlative conjunctions, and subordinating conjunctions. *She bought a gallon of milk and two dozen jelly doughnuts.*

context Literally meaning "with text," context refers to the situation in which something occurs, is spoken, or is written—in other words, the text that surrounds the text. The context of any given expression is vital for interpreting it.

contextual The adjective form of the noun *context* (see definition above).

contraction A contraction is a word with a letter or letters omitted, usually indicated by an apostrophe. *It's = It is.*

coordinating conjunction A coordinating conjunction joins two or more nouns, pronouns, verbs, adjectives, adverbs, prepositions, conjunctions, phrases, or clauses. Coordinating conjunctions include the words *and, but, or, nor, yet, for, so. He wanted to go bowling, but he preferred to see a movie.*

correlative conjunction A correlative conjunction is a paired conjunction that joins equal elements of a sentence: *both/and, not only/but also, just as/so, either/or, neither/nor, whether/or. Either he's telling the truth or he isn't.*

count noun Count nouns are used where it is reasonably possible to individually count the items that the noun names. *Who ate all the cookies?*

definite article The definite article *the* goes before a noun whose identity is expected to be known to the reader or is about to be revealed. In some cases, the noun is named earlier in the sentence. In other cases, the knowledge is inferred. You can also use *the* with superlative forms and with ordinal numerals (*the first, the sixth*). *The student looking at the map appears to be lost.* The phrase *looking at the map* tells which student the speaker is referring to, so *the* is used.

dependent clause A dependent clause cannot stand alone as a sentence. Often dependent clauses are independent clauses preceded by a subordinating conjunction. *After the ball game was over, we all went out to eat pizza.*

determiner Determiners are a class of modifiers and include the following common words: *a/an, the; this, these, that, those; my, our, your, his, her, its, their;* possessive nouns and noun phrases (*Emily's, her uncle's*); *whose, which, what; all, both, each, every, some, any, either, no, neither, many, more, most, much, (a) few, (a) little, several, enough;* the numerals *one, two, three,* and so on.

direct object A direct object is the noun, noun phrase, or pronoun that follows a transitive verb and receives the action of the verb. *The dog bit the intruder.*

formal speech/writing Formal speech and writing pay strict attention to grammatical standards and correct spelling, avoiding colloquial expressions and slang. Sentences may have a great deal of subordination. Formal writing, which is more likely to use longer words of Latin or Greek derivation than informal writing, appears in places such as academic journals and textbooks. You may hear formal speech in court cases or in speeches by public officials; these kinds of speeches are almost always written before they are delivered. Formal speech and writing require more attentiveness from both the writer and the reader or audience.

gerund A gerund is a noun derived from a verb ending in *-ing. Knitting is a relaxing and practical hobby.*

helping verb See *auxiliary verb.*

homonym Homonyms are words that sound alike but are spelled differently and have separate meanings. *They're waiting for their dinner to be served.*

idiomatic verb Idiomatic verbs require a specific preposition or prepositions to create a new meaning from the same base verb. These verbs are also called two-word or phrasal verbs. This class of verbs also includes those whose accompanying prepositions are less predictable. *She got over her illness quickly.* See Part 8, Prepositions, p. 145, for more examples of phrasal verbs and their particles.

imperative mood The imperative mood is used to give commands, make requests, and issue instructions. *Wash your hands before preparing food.*

indefinite article The indefinite article *a/an* is a kind of determiner that is used when the identity of the noun modified is not expected to be known to the reader, such as when a noun is introduced for the first time. *An* is a variant of *a* that goes directly before a word beginning with a vowel sound. *A strange man walked up to me on the street at night chewing an apple.*

independent clause An independent clause is one that contains a complete thought and can stand alone as a simple sentence.

indicative mood The indicative mood expresses statements of fact. Most kinds of speaking and writing are in the indicative mood. All three sentences in this entry are in the indicative mood, as are most of the sentences in this workbook.

indirect object An indirect object is a noun, noun phrase, or pronoun that follows a transitive verb and tells for whom/what or to whom/what the action is done. *Throw me the ball.*

infinitive The infinitive is the base form of the verb + *to*. You can use the infinitive in particular verbal phrases to state intentions, desires, or expectations. *I wanted <u>to watch</u> the homecoming parade from the balcony.*

informal speech/writing Informal speech and writing are conversational and colloquial. For example, a telephone conversation with a relative, an e-mail message sent to a friend, or a chat with the person sitting next to you on the bus will most likely be informal. This type of speech and writing bends—or sometimes entirely ignores—some of the grammar rules of English in order to create a kind of verbal shorthand: *Can't do much about it now* (explicit subject is missing). Generally, informal speech and writing feature shorter words rather than longer ones, and idiomatic expressions and slang are common.

intensive pronoun Intensive pronouns are created by adding *-self* or *-selves* to personal pronouns: *myself, yourself, himself, herself, itself, ourselves, yourselves,* and *themselves.* Intensive pronouns emphasize their antecedent. *I crocheted this sweater <u>myself</u>.*

intransitive verb An intransitive verb expresses action that is not directed toward a direct object. Such verbs are often followed by an adverb. *They <u>dressed</u> quickly.*

modal Modals are auxiliary verbs used most often in making requests and giving instructions. The nine most common modals are the pairs *can/could, will/would, shall/should, may/might,* and *must* (which has no pair). *<u>Would</u> you proofread my paper, please?*

modifier The word *modifier* comes from the verb *modify,* which means "to change in some way." Modifiers change the words they modify by describing them, limiting them, or making them more specific. *The chair*, for example, becomes *the green chair.* Even more specific would be *the green folding chair.*

mood Mood refers to how the speaker or writer intends a statement to be understood: as a fact (the indicative mood), as a command (the imperative mood), or as a desire, suggestion, or improbability (the subjunctive mood).

noncount noun A noncount noun names an item that is difficult or impossible to count. It does not have a plural. *Pour me a glass of <u>milk</u>, please.*

noun A noun is a word that names a person (*cousin*), place (*supermarket*), thing (*eraser*), or concept (*forgiveness*). Proper nouns name specific people, places, things, or concepts (*Oklahoma*). Collective nouns name groups (*team*). Nouns that have both singular and plural forms are called count nouns. Noncount nouns do not have a plural form.

noun clause A noun clause is a clause that functions as a noun within a sentence. You can use noun clauses to combine two sentences into one, with one sentence functioning as the independent clause and the other as a dependent clause embedded within the main sentence. *<u>That I spoke Spanish</u> proved to be very useful.*

object pronoun Object pronouns function as the object of a sentence, clause, or phrase. The object pronouns are *me, us, you, him, her, it, them, whom,* and *whomever. We bought <u>them</u> opera tickets.*

participle Participles are adjectives that have been created from verbs by adding suffixes, usually *-ed* and *-ing.* The **present participle** describes the thing or person causing the feeling or action. *The <u>terrifying</u> roller coaster ride made the girl fear for her life.* The **past participle** describes the person having the feeling or experiencing the action. *The <u>terrified</u> girl held on to the side of the roller coaster for dear life.*

phrasal verb See *idiomatic verb.*

phrasal-prepositional verb Phrasal-prepositional verbs are idiomatic verbs that combine *verb + adverbial particle + prepositional sequence* to create sentences such as *He just <u>gave up on</u> finishing his degree.*

phrase A phrase is a group of words expressing a coherent thought that does not include both a subject and a finite verb. Noun phrase: *A beautiful day.* Prepositional phrase: *To the museum.*

plural The form of a noun, verb, or pronoun that refers to more than one of something.

possessive pronoun Possessive pronouns show possession or ownership. The possessive pronouns are *my/mine, our/ours, your/your, his, her/hers, its, their/theirs,* and *whose/whosever. <u>Her</u> singing was beautiful.*

predicate A predicate is the part of a sentence that tells what the subject does. It consists of a verb and all its auxiliaries, modifiers, and complements.

predicate adjective A predicate adjective is an adjective that is separated from the noun it describes by a linking verb or another verb that functions similarly. *Something is <u>wrong</u> with the stove.*

preposition Prepositions are words that show the relationship between other words. Some of the most common prepositions are *in, on, at, to, from, by, for, of,* and *with.*

prepositional phrase A prepositional phrase is made up of a preposition followed by a noun or pronoun. *We took a cab <u>from the restaurant to the theater</u>.*

prepositional verb A prepositional verb is an idiomatic verb that requires a specific preposition or prepositions to be complete; it cannot stand alone without its proper preposition. *Wearing baggy pants is a fashion that <u>caught on</u> in the 1990s.*

pronoun A pronoun is a word that takes the place of a noun, another pronoun, or a phrase functioning as a noun. You can use pronouns to avoid repeating previously mentioned words. The word or group of words replaced by the pronoun is called the **antecedent**. Usually pronouns occur after the antecedent has already been stated, although they may also occur before the antecedent. Pronouns must agree with their antecedents in case, number, and gender.

reflexive pronoun A reflexive pronoun is created by adding *-self* or *-selves* to a personal pronoun: *myself, yourself, himself, herself, itself, ourselves, yourselves,* and *themselves.* Reflexive pronouns occur in the object position when the subject and object are the same. *Overcome with guilt, the criminal turned <u>himself</u> in.*

relative pronoun Relative pronouns link dependent clauses to independent clauses to form complete sentences from two separate ideas. The relative pronouns are *who, whom, whose, which,* and *that. The new supervisor, <u>who has just started work this week</u>, is feeling overwhelmed by the challenges of his new position.*

sentence A sentence is an independent clause punctuated as an individual unit. *He won $2,000 on a television game show.*

simple sentence A simple sentence is the most basic sentence in English, containing just a subject and a predicate. *She waved.*

singular The form of a noun, verb, or pronoun that refers to just one of something.

subject pronoun Subject pronouns function as the subject of a sentence or clause. The subject pronouns are *I, we, you, he, she, it, they, who,* and *whoever. <u>They</u> were going to the opera that evening.*

subject-verb-object word order The subject-verb-object word order is the most common in contemporary English statements. *She has a pet rabbit.* Questions in English are an exception: they place a verb before the subject. *<u>Does</u> she have a pet rabbit?*

subjunctive mood The subjunctive mood in English expresses a desire, suggestion, or improbability. The subjunctive is indicated by the form of the verb. *My mother asked that I <u>call</u> her when my plane lands.*

subordinating conjunction A subordinating conjunction introduces an adverb clause and indicates the relationship between the adverb clause and another clause (generally, an independent clause). *I liked dried pasta <u>until</u> I tasted fresh, homemade noodles.*

superlative form The superlative form is an adjective or adverb used in making comparisons among three or more things. Superlative adjectives usually end in *-est. That's the <u>smartest</u> cat I've ever seen.* Superlative adverbs are often formed from adjectives by adding the modifier *most* before the adjective. *He performed his work the <u>most diligently</u> of them all.*

tense Tense is the quality of a verb that indicates the time of action (or state of being) and type of action (or state of being). You can express tense through verb endings and auxiliary (helping) verbs. *She <u>goes</u> to the gym every day. She <u>went</u> to the gym yesterday. She <u>had gone</u> to the gym by the time I arrived home today. She <u>will have been going</u> to the gym for three consecutive months this Saturday.*

transitive verb A transitive verb expresses action directed toward a noun or pronoun (the direct object). *I <u>read</u> the book.*

two-word verb See *idiomatic verb.*

verb A verb is a word that shows action or a state of being. Verbs are used to join the subject to the rest of the sentence. *The boy <u>ran</u> across the street.*

voice, active and passive When referring to verbs, *voice* indicates whether the subject is acting (active voice) or being acted upon (passive voice). Active voice focuses on the agent responsible for the action in the sentence. Passive voice indicates that the acting agent is unknown or not of great importance in the context of the sentence. Passive voice can also be used deliberately to hide the agent responsible for the action. Active voice: *He <u>wrote</u> this book.* Passive voice: *This book was <u>written</u> by him.*

zero article The term *zero article* indicates the nonexistence of an article or a determiner in front of a noun. Zero article occurs only with noncount or plural count forms to signify general categories. *I'm afraid of <u>snakes</u>.* (There is no article or determiner in front of *snakes*.)

Appendix B
A Conjugated Verb

Conjugation of the Verb *Work*

Base form: work

Infinitive: to work

Present Tense

		Singular	Plural
First person		I work	we work
Second person		you work	you work
Third person	*masculine*	he works	they work
	feminine	she works	
	neuter	it works	

Past Tense

		Singular	Plural
First person		I worked	we worked
Second person		you worked	you worked
Third person	*masculine*	he worked	they worked
	feminine	she worked	
	neuter	it worked	

Future Tense

		Singular	Plural
First person		I will work	we will work
Second person		you will work	you will work
Third person	*masculine*	he will work	they will work
	feminine	she will work	
	neuter	it will work	

Present Progressive

		Singular	Plural
First person		I am working	we are working
Second person		you are working	you are working
Third person	*masculine*	he is working	they are working
	feminine	she is working	
	neuter	it is working	

Past Progressive

		Singular	Plural
First person		I was working	we were working
Second person		you were working	you were working
Third person	*masculine*	he was working	they were working
	feminine	she was working	
	neuter	it was working	

Future Progressive

		Singular	Plural
First person		I will be working	we will be working
Second person		you will be working	you will be working
Third person	*masculine*	he will be working	they will be working
	feminine	she will be working	
	neuter	it will be working	

Present Perfect

		Singular	Plural
First person		I have worked	we have worked
Second person		you have worked	you have worked
Third person	*masculine*	he has worked	they have worked
	feminine	she has worked	
	neuter	it has worked	

Past Perfect

		Singular	Plural
First person		I had worked	we had worked
Second person		you had worked	you had worked
Third person	*masculine*	he had worked	they had worked
	feminine	she had worked	
	neuter	it had worked	

Future Perfect

		Singular	Plural
First person		I will have worked	we will have worked
Second person		you will have worked	you will have worked
Third person	*masculine*	he will have worked	they will have worked
	feminine	she will have worked	
	neuter	it will have worked	

Present Perfect Progressive

		Singular	Plural
First person		I have been working	we have been working
Second person		you have been working	you have been working
Third person	*masculine*	he has been working	they have been working
	feminine	she has been working	
	neuter	it has been working	

Past Perfect Progressive

		Singular	Plural
First person		I had been working	we had been working
Second person		you had been working	you had been working
Third person	*masculine*	he had been working	they had been working
	feminine	she had been working	
	neuter	it had been working	

Future Perfect Progressive

		Singular	Plural
First person		I will have been working	we will have been working
Second person		you will have been working	you will have been working
Third person	*masculine*	he will have been working	they will have been working
	feminine	she will have been working	
	neuter	it will have been working	

Appendix C
Commonly Used Idiomatic Verbs

Be about to   be ready or prepared to do something; be on the verge of doing something

I am about to go to the grocery store; do you need anything there?

Be off   go away; leave

We have to load just one more bag and then we'll be off.

Be on to   find out about something or someone

My father was on to our plans to throw him a surprise party.

Catch on   to become popular; to understand something

You might feel lost at first, but you will soon catch on.

Caught on   past tense of *catch on*

The idea of cell phones caught on a long time ago.

Clear up   resolve or solve a problem; explain something previously misunderstood

We cleared up the misunderstanding quickly once we were able to talk in person.

Close down   not operate any longer; go out of business; also **shut down**

The clothing store closed down because it wasn't getting enough business.

Come across   find; discover

While going through her grandmother's closet, she came across a beautiful old fur coat.

Come back   return

I hope you'll come back soon.

Come up   be mentioned

If your name comes up during the meeting, I'll be sure to explain why you're not there.

Come up with   create; think of

Our brainstorming session helped us come up with some great ideas.

Dress up   wear nice, formal clothing

Some people like to dress up when they go to an expensive restaurant.

Drop in   (sometimes **drop by**) visit for a brief period of time, sometimes unexpectedly

He just dropped in to discuss the progress we've made on his project.

End up   become; conclude; finish (a certain result is usually specified). See also **turn out**.

The company ended up bankrupt because of unethical business practices.

Figure out   determine or understand something; solve a problem

> She couldn't figure out what he was trying to say.

Get away with   escape with no punishment

> He'll never get away with his crimes.

Get over   recover

> I hope he gets over his pneumonia soon.

Get (something) out of   receive a benefit or profit from something in some way

> Stockholders hope to get something out of their financial investments.

Get through   survive; endure

> We did our best to get through the tragedy.

Go along with   agree with or participate in something

> I'm not going along with his pranks anymore.

Hang around   be someplace or near someplace (or someone)

> The boys were hanging around the kitchen hoping dinner would be ready soon.

Hang on   wait

> Hang on, and I'll help you when I've finished washing the dishes.

Hang out   spend time somewhere or with someone

> We always hang out at the lake after school.

Hang with   keep listening; keep paying attention to what someone is saying. See also **stick with**.

> Are you hanging with me?

Laid out   established

> The company laid out its policy on tardiness.

Look forward to   anticipate

> I look forward to seeing you soon.

Make out   understand

> There was so much interference on the cell phone that I couldn't make out what my friend was saying.

Make up   create; invent; lie

> We need to make up some guidelines for using the photocopier.

Make up for   compensate or atone for something

> I made my husband chocolate chip cookies to make up for dropping his birthday cake.

Put off   delay doing something; be offended or annoyed by someone

> I put off doing my homework too long, and now I have to stay up late to finish it.

> He was put off by her casual attitude about their collaborative project.

Put on   dress oneself in something (article of clothing)

> I put on my hat, coat, and gloves and went outside.

Put up with   endure; tolerate

   I'm not putting up with your silliness any longer.

Run into   meet unexpectedly

   I ran into my neighbor while shopping at the mall.

Set out   leave (for a particular destination)

   The fishermen set out early the next morning.

Slip up   make a mistake

   I'm afraid I might slip up and say the wrong thing to him.

Start over   do something again from the beginning

   When his building plans were not approved by the city, the contractor had to start over.

Stick with   (sometimes **hang with**) persevere with something or someone; continue doing something or continue being with someone

   Just stick with your English studies, and little by little it will get easier.

Take after   resemble; look like

   She takes after her mother more than her father.

Take down   transcribe something dictated; write something on paper; take notes

   Take down this address, please.

Take off   depart; leave; remove

   The plane took off.

   Please take off your hat indoors.

Take on   accept

   My sister always takes on more than she can possibly do.

Think back to   remember; recall

   When I think back to my younger days, I wonder where all that youthful energy went!

Throw up   vomit. This expression is considered more polite than saying *vomit*.

   After drinking too much milk, the baby threw up.

Tried out   made a trial of; experimented with; tried something for a period of time

   He tried out that new restaurant but found the food too spicy for his taste.

Turn off   give a negative impression; annoy

   The unprofessional behavior of the sales associate turned the customer off.

Turn out   conclude; finish (a certain result is usually specified). See also **end up**.

   The high school musical turned out very well.

Wake up   awaken; stop sleeping

   I wake up every morning at 7 A.M.

Appendix D
ESL Resources Online

Bedford/St. Martin's offers an extensive collection of exercises on the Exercise Central Web site: http://www.bedfordstmartins.com/exercisecentral/

In addition, the *Re:Writing* Web site contains interactive exercises that target ESL trouble spots: http://bcs.bedfordstmartins.com/rewriting/ge3.html

Additional ESL resources may also be found on the Web at the addresses listed below:

General

Purdue Online Writing Lab—ESL Resources
http://owl.english.purdue.edu/handouts/esl/index.html

English Language Center Study Zone from the University of Victoria
http://web2.uvcs.uvic.ca/elc/studyzone/grammar.htm

Guide to Grammar and Writing by the Capital Community College Foundation
http://grammar.ccc.commnet.edu/grammar

Quizzes, Games, Podcasts, and Other Interactive Resources

Activities for ESL Students
http://a4esl.org/

Grammar Bytes!
http://www.chompchomp.com/

Interesting Things for ESL Students
http://www.manythings.org/

Randall's ESL Cyber Listening Lab
http://www.esl-lab.com/

ESL Podcast
http://www.eslpod.com/

Grammar Girl
http://grammar.quickanddirtytips.com/

Discussion Boards

Dave's ESL Café
http://www.eslcafe.com/

EnglishForums.com

http://www.englishforums.com

Reference Tools

Babelfish Translation

http://babelfish.altavista.com/

Merriam-Webster Online

http://www.m-w.com/

Appendix E
Answers to Exercise Items

Part 1 Nouns

EXERCISE 1.1 Singular and Plural Nouns

1. immigrants 2. ocean 3. countries 4. corners 5. land 6. ports 7. tests 8. diseases 9. letters 10. officials

EXERCISE 1.2 Singular and Plural Nouns

1. The Beatles were one of the most popular musical **acts** of all time. 2. Four young **men** from Liverpool, England, made a fortune playing songs that young people loved. 3. Recordings by the Beatles still sell millions of **copies** today. 4. Some buyers are middle-aged fans who have not lost **respect** for the group. 5. Correct. 6. Playing **music** from their youth makes some fans feel young again. 7. Other people who buy Beatles records are **teenagers** discovering the songs for the first time. 8. Even today, a teenager is likely to know bits of Beatle **trivia**. 9. Some young listeners become fans, but others don't understand the **fuss** about the Beatles. 10. The two surviving Beatles are in their mid-sixties, but their fans span all **ages**.

EXERCISE 1.3 Singular and Plural Nouns

1. agency 2. attempts 3. role 4. mail 5. pack 6. communication 7. president 8. country 9. train 10. times

EXERCISE 1.4 Count and Noncount Nouns

1. number 2. reasons 3. freedom 4. families 5. Overpopulation 6. discrimination 7. battles 8. Legislation 9. benefits 10. advice

EXERCISE 1.5 Count and Noncount Nouns

Hawaii is a chain of **(1.) islands** in the Pacific Ocean. The warm **(2.) weather** brings visitors from all over the world. The abundance of **(3.) fruit** is also an attraction; there's nothing like eating a fresh **(4.) pineapple** for breakfast. Another attraction is the natural beauty of Hawaii's geographical **(5.) features** such as volcanoes, waterfalls, and beaches. Enjoying the natural beauty is a great way to find **(6.) relief** from a hectic lifestyle. Hawaii also has many natural **(7.) resources**. One of them is **(8.) coffee**. Visitors will also find many spas promoting **(9.) relaxation**. Certainly, Hawaii has inspired many **(10.) people** to visit again.

Part 2 Articles

EXERCISE 2.1 Articles

1. A 2. the 3. the OR X 4. the 5. a 6. the OR X 7. A OR The 8. an 9. the 10. an

EXERCISE 2.2 Articles

1. The U.S. Constitution guarantees freedom of religion to all residents of the country. 2. Correct 3. Instead, by law, all residents are allowed to worship as they please or to choose not to worship at all. 4. The U.S. Supreme Court declared school prayer unconstitutional about forty years ago. 5. Correct 6. Correct 7. Teachers or other authority figures in a school may not legally lead prayers in class or at school functions. 8. Correct 9. The U.S. Constitution

does not restrict the practice of personal religious beliefs. **10.** But the law does not permit the use of class time in public schools for group expression of a particular faith.

EXERCISE 2.3 Articles

1. the **2.** a **3.** the **4.** the **5.** A **6.** A **7.** a **8.** an **9.** a **10.** a

EXERCISE 2.4 Articles

1. Correct **2.** Most students never read beyond **the** first page of **a** homework assignment in a textbook. But there are many useful parts to **a** book. **3.** Correct **4.** Correct **5.** There is usually an appendix after the assignments that gives you useful information such as **a** dictionary or **a** glossary of terms used in the textbook. **6.** At the end of the book, there is **an** index. This is an alphabetical list of all the topics in the book and their page number. **7.** Correct **8.** Correct **9.** Correct **10.** In the end, it is still a textbook, and **the** only page that matters to the student is the homework assignment.

Part 3 Pronouns

EXERCISE 3.1 Personal Pronouns

1. you **2.** You **3.** They **4.** they **5.** they **6.** you **7.** We **8.** I **9.** they **10.** They

EXERCISE 3.2 Personal Pronouns

1. he **2.** he **3.** they; He **4.** they **5.** She **6.** he **7.** it **8.** it OR he **9.** he **10.** It

EXERCISE 3.3 Personal Pronouns

1. It **2.** They **3.** it **4.** they **5.** We **6.** I **7.** they **8.** it **9.** She **10.** he

EXERCISE 3.4 Object Pronouns

1. him **2.** it **3.** her **4.** him **5.** her **6.** it **7.** him **8.** it **9.** him **10.** them

EXERCISE 3.5 Object Pronouns

1. them **2.** them **3.** him **4.** her **5.** them **6.** it **7.** you **8.** me **9.** me **10.** them

EXERCISE 3.6 Object Pronouns

1. me **2.** them **3.** it **4.** me **5.** me; it **6.** me; him **7.** It **8.** her **9.** me **10.** it

EXERCISE 3.7 Possessive Pronouns

1. his **2.** his **3.** her **4.** her **5.** his **6.** its; his **7.** his **8.** their **9.** their **10.** our

EXERCISE 3.8 Possessive Pronouns

1. his; his **2.** their **3.** her **4.** his **5.** his **6.** her **7.** her **8.** their **9.** his **10.** its

EXERCISE 3.9 Possessive Pronouns

1. my **2.** our **3.** her **4.** his **5.** our **6.** my **7.** my **8.** my **9.** their **10.** my

EXERCISE 3.10 Object/Possessive Pronouns

1. their **2.** their **3.** my **4.** their; them **5.** me **6.** his **7.** me **8.** my **9.** it **10.** your

EXERCISE 3.11 Object/Possessive Pronouns

1. my **2.** me; him; our **3.** you; mine **4.** me; them **5.** him; us **6.** me; her **7.** him **8.** him; me **9.** him; ours **10.** it

EXERCISE 3.12 Object/Possessive Pronouns

1. their **2.** their **3.** him **4.** her **5.** them **6.** his **7.** your **8.** you **9.** your **10.** them **11.** their

EXERCISE 3.13 Reflexive/Intensive Pronouns

1. herself 2. himself 3. herself 4. themselves 5. himself 6. yourself 7. myself 8. himself 9. ourselves 10. yourselves

EXERCISE 3.14 Reflexive/Intensive Pronouns

1. themselves 2. myself 3. herself 4. ourselves 5. themselves 6. himself 7. herself 8. myself 9. oneself 10. myself

EXERCISE 3.15 Reflexive/Intensive Pronouns

1. myself 2. herself 3. themselves 4. herself 5. himself 6. ourselves 7. themselves 8. herself 9. himself 10. myself

EXERCISE 3.16 Relative Pronouns

1. whom 2. whom 3. that 4. which 5. which 6. that 7. which 8. which 9. that 10. whom

EXERCISE 3.17 Relative Pronouns

1. which 2. whom 3. that 4. that 5. whom 6. that 7. which 8. that 9. whom 10. that (for answers 2, 5, and 9 *who* would also be correct in informal situations)

EXERCISE 3.18 Relative Pronouns

Possible Answers 1. The Taj Mahal is a monument **that** is considered one of the most beautiful sites in the world. **2.** The Taj Mahal is a memorial **that** King Shah Jahan built for his queen, Mumtaz Mahal. **3.** It is also an ancient mausoleum **that** holds the tomb of Mumtaz Mahal. **4.** King Shah Jahan wanted to show his deep love for Mumtaz Mahal, **who** died during childbirth. **5.** The King decreed that the Taj Mahal be built in a special location **that** had to be both scenic and close to his palace. **6.** The King wanted to build a monument **that** no one would ever forget. **7.** Shah Jahan selected skilled architects and masons **who** came from all over India and the Middle East. **8.** The Taj Mahal is made of marble, precious stones, and gems, **which** made it a very expensive project. **9.** Every year, the Taj Mahal attracts millions of visitors **who** are always surprised at the grandeur and size of the monument. **10.** The Taj Mahal is an extraordinary monument **that** is a testimony to the deep love Shah Jahan had for his wife.

Part 4 Negative Statements and Questions

EXERCISE 4.1 Negative Statements

1. In my first year of college, most of my friends **did not choose** to study one of the romance languages. **2.** More recently, languages such as Chinese or Japanese **have not been** more popular. **3.** Studying a new language in the early morning **has not been** satisfying. **4.** I **did not learn** several thousand kanji characters. **5.** Learning the kanji characters also **did not help** me learn Japanese. **6.** The Japanese language **does not use** kanji characters in its written language. **7.** I **did not practice** speaking Chinese with native speakers at my college. **8.** They **did not say** that they understood me. **9.** I **do not believe** they were telling me the truth. **10.** I **did not love** learning and speaking another language.

EXERCISE 4.2 Negative Statements

1. Telecommuting, which refers to working at home, is not supported by my boss. **2.** My boss does not allow every employee in our company to telecommute at least one day per week. **3.** Traffic in our area is not very bad, so telecommuting is not needed to help reduce the number of cars on the road. **4.** My boss does not feel that telecommuting improves the attitude of employees. OR My boss feels that telecommuting does not improve the attitude of employees.

5. He also does not think that if employees' attitudes are good they will work harder. **6.** Therefore, my boss believes that telecommuting does not result in higher productivity. OR Therefore, my boss does not believe that telecommuting results in higher productivity. **7.** My boss does not allow any employees to telecommute more than one day a week. OR My boss does not allow employees to telecommute on any days of the week. **8.** He does not allow any employees to telecommute more than one day, even though some employees live far away from our office. **9.** My boss does not think that in the future any employee will work from home on any days of the week. OR My boss thinks that in the future no employees will work from home on any days of the week. **10.** I do not like my boss because he does not allow telecommuting.

EXERCISE 4.3 Negative Statements

1. Before the invention of the modern airplane, people **did not travel** by car or railway. **2.** People **did not own** only one car for road trips. **3.** Better highways **were not constructed** as more and more people traveled by car. **4.** The railway **did not provide** an alternate mode of traveling. **5.** Railway trains **did not offer** luxury accommodations such as sleeping cabins and fine restaurants. **6.** People also **did not find** a way to travel overseas: luxury cruise ships. **7.** Cruise ship operators **did not take** into account the length of the journey in their plans. **8.** Airlines also **did not begin** offering luxury accommodations such as first class seats and hot meals on flights. **9.** Some airlines even **did not have** fully reclining seats and televisions for each passenger. **10.** Perhaps one day there **will not be** gyms on airplanes!

EXERCISE 4.4 Negative Statements

1. Van Gogh **did not learn** to paint as a young man. **2.** His paintings **cannot be seen** in museums around the world. **3.** He **is not best known** for his textured brush strokes. **4.** He **did not paint** with oil paints to produce rich scenes of nature. **5.** Van Gogh **was not close** to his brother, Theo. **6.** He **did not suffer** from depression and an addiction to absinthe. **7.** Those two afflictions **did not make** his paintings more intense. **8.** He **did not die** just around the time his artwork was becoming famous. **9.** Many collectors and museums **have not bought** his paintings. **10.** Van Gogh's famous painting of sunflowers **did not sell** for millions of dollars.

EXERCISE 4.5 Questions

1. Were the Beatles from Liverpool, England? **2.** Were there four musicians in the band? **3.** Did Paul McCartney and John Lennon write many of the songs? **4.** Was the band's first successful single "Love Me Do"? **5.** Is the term for the crazed obsession with the Beatles called "Beatlemania"? **6.** Did the band perform on the *Ed Sullivan Show* in the United States in February 1964? **7.** Did they also star in the movie *A Hard Day's Night*? **8.** Was John Lennon's wife's name Yoko Ono? **9.** Was the band's last performance in San Francisco? **10.** Did the band officially break up in 1970?

EXERCISE 4.6 Questions

1. Did your cousin graduate from law school on Saturday? **2.** Is his area of concentration Business Law? **3.** Was his undergraduate degree in history? **4.** Did he choose history because it seemed like a good pre-law degree? **5.** Were there 150 students who graduated with him? **6.** Is the law school located in southern Florida? **7.** Does he plan to take the bar exam in July? **8.** Would he like to move to Washington, D.C.? **9.** Does he plan to move with his best friend? **10.** Does he want to live in Washington, D.C., because it has so many opportunities?

EXERCISE 4.7 Questions

Possible Answers 1. When does the summer Olympics take place? **2.** What sporting events does the Olympics feature? **3.** Who competes in the events, and what do they compete for? **4.** Where did the summer Olympics of 2008 take place? **5.** When did the first modern

Olympic Games take place? **6.** What is the decathlon? **7.** How long is the marathon? **8.** Why did the United States boycott the Olympics in 1980? **9.** Why did the Soviet Union boycott the Olympics in 1984? **10.** What do the five rings on the Olympic flag represent?

EXERCISE 4.8 Questions

Possible Answers 1. What is the awards ceremony for the motion picture industry called? **2.** Why was the awards ceremony created? **3.** Where does the ceremony take place? **4.** When does the ceremony usually take place? **5.** Who sees the ceremony on TV? **6.** What do celebrities wear to the ceremony? **7.** What are the most popular categories? **8.** Which film won ten awards in 2004? **9.** Who won the most awards for a male actor in Academy history? **10.** What are the Academy Awards becoming more famous for?

Part 5 Sentences and Clauses

EXERCISE 5.1 Sentence Subjects

1. X **2.** It **3.** it **4.** it **5.** There **6.** it **7.** X **8.** There **9.** it **10.** there

EXERCISE 5.2 Word Order in Sentences

1. Many people **believe** that too much sex and violence is shown on television. **2.** Most parents would **like** to monitor their children's television viewing. **3.** For many people, however, keeping track of a child's choice of television programs **is** impossible. **4.** One solution might **come** from recent technological innovations. **5.** Several years ago, American television manufacturers **agreed** to start equipping all new televisions with a V-chip. **6.** The V **stands** for "violence." **7.** The V-chip **screens** out shows that contain sex and violence. **8.** Parents **program** the chip to block shows with certain ratings. **9.** With the V-chip, individuals, not the government, **censor** their children's television programs. **10.** Of course, today, many children **know** better than their parents how to program electronic devices.

EXERCISE 5.3 Word Order in Sentences

Possible Answers 1. The television industry provides ratings for television programs so that parents can decide what to allow their children to watch. **2.** The ratings system is similar to the one used for movies. **3.** The ratings system exists already, but people get a V-chip only when they buy a new television. **4.** Older children might be attracted to programming rated as explicit. **5.** Most parents know that kids want what they are not allowed to have. **6.** Parents with an older television will not be able to block out shows rated for mature audiences. **7.** Some critics say that it is only a matter of time before a child learns to tamper with the V-chip programmer. **8.** Advertisers worry that parents will block out the prime-time shows that generate the most advertising revenue. **9.** If a show has an explicit rating, parents might block it out and advertisers might shy away. **10.** The television industry argues that the V-chip is a kind of censorship since it will indirectly control the kinds of shows produced.

EXERCISE 5.4 Compound Sentences

1. William Rosenberg opened the first Dunkin' Donuts shop in Quincy, Massachusetts, in 1948, and that store still stands today. **2.** Dunkin' Donuts has always sold donuts, but it has sold more coffee than donuts in the last few years. **3.** Dunkin' Donuts has grown to over 7,000 stores today, and (but) the company has plans for more growth. **4.** The first Starbucks was opened in 1971 in Seattle, Washington, and that store is still open today. **5.** The original plan for Starbucks was to sell coffee beans and coffee-brewing equipment, but in 1983, an employee in the company, Howard Schultz, encouraged the owners to sell coffee drinks as well. **6.** The original owners thought that the main focus should be beans and equipment, so they did not take Schultz's advice. **7.** Schultz started his own coffee shop, for he knew that the business would succeed because Americans would buy coffee drinks and not just beans. **8.** The original owners sold their chain of Starbucks stores to Schultz in 1987, and Schultz immediately increased the number of stores. **9.** Today, both Dunkin' Donuts and Starbucks are keen competitors for the coffee market, yet in many ways, the two shops are quite different. **10.** Dunkin' Donuts is said to have a blue-collar customer base, and (but) Starbucks is said to have a white-collar customer base.

EXERCISE 5.5 Complex Sentences

Answers will vary.

EXERCISE 5.6 Noun Clauses

1. We don't really know who invented the Internet. **2.** I am not really sure when people started buying personal computers. **3.** I wonder to whom the first e-mail message was written. **4.** It would be interesting to find out what the first e-mail message said. **5.** We don't know where the first personal computer was built. **6.** It's difficult to determine if computers will become less expensive than books in the future. **7.** Yes, I believe that Bill Gates made his money in computers. **8.** You would have to ask Bill Gates if he has more money than Warren Buffet. **9.** I don't know how big Bill Gates's house is. **10.** That's a good question. I wonder if Michael Jordan ever made more money than Bill Gates.

EXERCISE 5.7 Noun Clauses

Possible Answers 1. It is a new airline regulation that passengers can now only bring one piece of luggage and a hand-held bag into the airplane cabin. **2.** It is now mandatory that the piece of luggage meet the new overhead bin size requirements and the hand-held bag fit completely under the seat. **3.** It was often the case that travelers couldn't fit everything they needed for a business trip into these small bags. **4.** Travelers had to hand over as checked luggage whichever bags exceeded size restrictions. **5.** It irritated many passengers that the airlines often lost checked baggage. **6.** In addition, it often interferes with busy travelers' schedules that checked bags take a long time to arrive at the baggage claim. **7.** It is encouraging that the airlines have been looking for solutions to this problem. **8.** Major airlines have suggested that airplanes should increase the amount of space available in overhead bins so that passengers can bring more and larger carry-ons. **9.** Recent studies have shown that airplanes can achieve departure six to eight minutes faster with the larger bins. **10.** It is uncertain whether flight attendants will be happy about this change.

EXERCISE 5.8 Noun Clauses

Possible Answers 1. It is evident why some companies are becoming concerned about what their employees are doing. **2.** Systems administrators can use software to see the amount of e-mail that employees send and receive each day. **3.** Is it necessary for the company to know that an employee e-mails jokes from a business computer? **4.** It could be considered a breach of privacy when managers read employees' e-mail. **5.** One employee said that she would sue her company for breach of privacy. **6.** The systems administrator tells employees that it is his job to prevent problems. **7.** There are many reasons that cause managers to install monitoring software. **8.** It is true that companies have to buy more bandwidth if their employees send huge amounts of e-mail. **9.** Lower-level employees are concerned whenever their e-mail is scrutinized but senior executives' e-mail is not. **10.** It is important that managers create an atmosphere that makes employees feel trusted and fairly treated.

EXERCISE 5.9 Adjective Clauses

Possible Answers 1. I spoke to a surgeon who said that plastic surgery is sometimes a parent's idea rather than a teen's. **2.** However, more often the teenager is the one who convinces the parent to pay for procedures. **3.** High school can be a harsh environment in which the slightest physical imperfections can provoke torment and teasing. **4.** Media images of young men and women to which teens are frequently exposed show impossibly perfect faces and bodies. OR Teens are frequently exposed to media images of young men and women that show impossibly perfect faces and bodies. **5.** Like it or not, we are living in a superficial culture in which attractive people get better treatment than unattractive people. **6.** Therefore, people whose bodies aren't even fully developed are requesting plastic surgery. **7.** One woman who was insistent about changing her appearance went to a plastic surgeon's office. **8.** She demanded to have the wrinkles that were around her eyes removed. **9.** There were just two problems, which the surgeon pointed out to her. **10.** The problems, which prevented her from having the surgery, were that she was nineteen years old and that she had no wrinkles. OR The problems, which were that she was nineteen years old and that she had no wrinkles, prevented her from having the surgery.

EXERCISE 5.10 Adjective Clauses

Possible Answers Nowadays, there are several Internet sites that [delete **they**] show live broadcasts of cosmetic surgery. If people miss the live coverage, they can pull up archival video footage in **which** patients undergo procedures from liposuction to facelifts. This new trend shows that plastic surgery has gone from something **that** was considered shameful or vain to something **that** is considered normal or even a status symbol. The ten million Americans who had plastic surgery in the 1990s represent every social stratum. Moreover, the majority of Americans **who** had plastic surgery came from households that [delete **they**] earned below $60,000. The popularity of the Web casts also demonstrates how much people love to watch live procedures **in** which there is a lot of blood and gore. How do patients feel about being the subject of broadcasts in **which** their bodies are sliced open? Apparently, just fine; the procedures, **which** are free for patients who model for Web casts, attract hundreds of e-mails per day from candidates.

EXERCISE 5.11 Adverb Clauses

1. that **2.** Since **3.** as much as **4.** Just as **5.** although **6.** although **7.** Whenever **8.** When **9.** since **10.** Because

EXERCISE 5.12 Adverb Clauses

1. When Andy woke up this morning, he looked out the window. **2.** As he looked at his car in the driveway, he noticed that his tire looked very low. **3.** Andy thought this was strange because he had just gotten new tires the previous week. **4.** As soon as he finished his breakfast, he went out to his car to take a look. **5.** As he came closer to his car, he realized that he had a flat tire. **6.** After he had taken off the flat tire and had put on his spare tire, he drove to his mechanic's shop to get the flat tire replaced. **7.** Because he had a warranty on his new tires, the mechanic replaced the tire at no charge. **8.** While the mechanic was taking off the flat tire, he noticed a nail sticking into the rubber. **9.** When Andy saw the nail, he realized that he must have gotten the flat tire the night before while driving through a junkyard. **10.** A flat tire was distressing to Andy because he had an important exam at school this morning.

EXERCISE 5.13 Conditional Sentences

1. had **2.** not watch **3.** were **4.** were **5.** would not take **6.** are **7.** were **8.** turn **9.** isn't **10.** becomes

EXERCISE 5.14 Conditional Sentences

Possible Answers 1. wants **2.** receive (OR will receive) **3.** appear (OR will appear) **4.** want **5.** wanted **6.** would sell **7.** would start **8.** had believed **9.** does not plan **10.** would have filled out (OR would fill out) **11.** use **12.** are **13.** will think **14.** were **15.** do not have **16.** may end up

Part 6 Verbs

EXERCISE 6.1 Simple Present Tense

1. means 2. knows 3. swim 4. occurs 5. happen 6. wish 7. believe 8. foretell 9. take 10. thank

EXERCISE 6.2 Simple Past Tense

1. crashed 2. thought 3. captured 4. dared 5. left 6. knew 7. came 8. reached 9. found 10. discovered

EXERCISE 6.3 Present and Past Tenses

1. went 2. remember 3. became 4. was 5. lie 6. repeated 7. was 8. graduated 9. started 10. take

EXERCISE 6.4 Present and Past Tenses

1. In 2002, my eighth-grade teacher told us we **had** to take our state's mandated math and reading tests at the end of the school year. 2. My teacher **spent** the whole spring of 2003 drilling us on the practice tests. 3. School officials came to our class and reassured us that we could not pass or **fail** the test. Scores were for school statistics only. 4. Instead, they said that our school and the teachers **were** being tested. 5. The students agreed that nobody **was** fooled by the officials' remarks. 6. My friend Hector said, "The test results **are** going to be sent to our parents." 7. In May of that year, we **sat** in class every day for a week completing the test. 8. I **scored** in the fiftieth percentile, so my results were exactly average. 9. Now I think of those results and **remember** the eighth grade fondly. 10. I still believe that kids **learn** more in school when less time is spent on test preparation.

EXERCISE 6.5 Present Perfect Tense

1. have begun 2. have been 3. have not driven 4. have taken 5. have heard 6. have told 7. have said 8. have heard 9. have mentioned 10. have waited

EXERCISE 6.6 Present Perfect Tense

1. spoken 2. become 3. forbidden 4. drawn 5. left 6. led 7. held 8. written 9. begun 10. made

EXERCISE 6.7 Past Perfect Tense

1. had had 2. had become 3. had become 4. had been 5. had impressed 6. had seen 7. had helped; had become 8. had visited 9. had had; had not been 10. had taken off 11. had lost 12. had accumulated; had acquired; had won 13. had been

EXERCISE 6.8 Future Perfect Tense

1. will have been published OR will be published 2. will have read 3. will have bought 4. will have become 5. will have obtained 6. will have gotten 7. will have forgotten 8. will have been equipped OR will be equipped 9. will have reached 10. will have become

EXERCISE 6.9 Perfect Tenses

1. has been considering; present perfect 2. will have spent; future perfect 3. had served; past perfect 4. will have provided; future perfect 5. had hoped; past perfect 6. has tried; present perfect 7. has dreamed; present perfect 8. had wanted; past perfect 9. has assured; present perfect 10. will have decided; future perfect

EXERCISE 6.10 Progressive Tenses

1. has been teaching 2. has been receiving 3. was noticing 4. is hoping 5. had been visiting 6. are hunting 7. will be looking 8. are wishing 9. is looking 10. is wondering

EXERCISE 6.11 Active and Passive Voice

1. was invented 2. be developed 3. needed 4. is given 5. selected 6. were using 7. developed 8. began 9. can be called 10. was made

EXERCISE 6.12 Active and Passive Voice

1. analyzes 2. was released; were published 3. took; had made 4. are causing 5. be sub-contracted 6. allows 7. will be eliminated OR have been eliminated 8. be updated 9. be encouraged 10. has generated

EXERCISE 6.13 Modals

1. would 2. can 3. would 4. can 5. might 6. should 7. could 8. would 9. would; might 10. Will

EXERCISE 6.14 Modals

1. I soon discovered that I **had to** choose a major after two years of coursework. 2. I **couldn't** decide what career field interested me most, so selecting a major was difficult. 3. At the beginning of my third year of coursework, I **had to** make a choice. 4. My adviser told me that I **could** change my mind later if I decided I wasn't happy with my decision. 5. I decided that I **would** study engineering. 6. When I took my first engineering course, I discovered that I **couldn't** understand some of the math required to complete my homework assignments. 7. I realized that I **should** have taken more advanced math courses to prepare for my engineering classes. 8. Now I am taking an extra math course to catch up, and I **should** finish my engineering degree next spring. 9. I **couldn't** wait until I started work as an engineer. 10. In the meantime, my professors tell me that I **should** study diligently to prepare for my career.

EXERCISE 6.15 Modals

Possible Answers 1. would have studied **2.** had to struggle **3.** would have considered (OR might have considered) **4.** would have stayed (OR might have stayed) **5.** had to venture (OR should venture) **6.** can enjoy (OR will enjoy) **7.** would have (OR might have) **8.** would feel (OR might feel) **9.** would miss (OR might miss) **10.** will prepare (OR can prepare)

EXERCISE 6.16 *To be* Verbs

1. is 2. are 3. is 4. was 5. were 6. are 7. were 8. are 9. am 10. am

EXERCISE 6.17 *To be* Verbs

1. was 2. were 3. was 4. be 5. were 6. is 7. is 8. am 9. was 10. is

EXERCISE 6.18 Verb Phrases

1. regarded 2. learned 3. face 4. are trying 5. asked 6. involve 7. volunteer 8. believe 9. achieve 10. united

EXERCISE 6.19 Verb Phrases

Possible Answers 1. Students of English **are** often **surprised** by the differences between written and conversational English. **2.** Those students who **have studied** formal written English may find conversational English difficult to understand. **3.** Students who **have** recently **come** to an English-speaking country may have particular trouble with slang vocabulary and expressions. **4.** Conversation classes in English **are supposed** to help students become familiar with spoken English by simulating real-life situational dialogues. **5.** Students who **have** not **been exposed** to spoken English can listen to English radio or TV broadcasts to help them learn English. **6.** Just listening to spoken English **can be useful** in learning oral speech patterns and intonation. **7.** Many students find that listening to songs with English lyrics **can help** them learn new vocabulary and expressions. OR Many students find that listening to songs with English lyrics **helps** them learn new vocabulary and expressions. **8.** Some students who **do** not **feel** a need to learn spoken English might prefer to listen to radio broadcasts in their native language rather than broadcasts in English. **9.** If such students do not make a great effort to learn conversational English, they **may** never **understand** the spoken language well. **10.** Students in English classes who **may** not **have been working** hard on learning spoken English need to understand that an inability to speak and understand English can limit their opportunities.

EXERCISE 6.20 Simple, Perfect, and Progressive Verb Phrases

While I **was shopping** at a grocery store last week, I **counted** five different brands of bottled water on the shelves. These days, bottled water **costs** more than carbonated beverages, but many consumers now **feel** that good health is worth the greater price.

Nutrition experts **have observed** that Americans **consume** too much soda and junk food. Prior to these findings, some parents **noticed** that their children were more sluggish and inattentive after they **had eaten** junk food. In many cases, they **had been snacking** at school.

Now nutrition experts insist that children **need** breakfast before school so that they **do not stop** at vending machines for sodas or greasy snacks. Because studies **have shown** that students perform better when they eat nutritious foods, some schools **are considering** a ban on certain junk foods and soda machines.

However, many parents **believe** that good nutrition should be enforced by parents, not schools. They **resent** being told by the school administration what not to put in their children's lunch. Based on recent sales of bottled water, it **appears** that consumers **are making** better nutritional choices.

EXERCISE 6.21 Simple, Perfect, and Progressive Verb Phrases

Possible Answers 1. Since then, the states **have** often **challenged** the federal government either by ignoring or refusing to implement the decision or by filing court cases. **2.** The case of Central High School in Little Rock, Arkansas, **is** one of the most famous examples of a state fighting this federal mandate. **3.** When the school **opened** in September 1957, the Arkansas National Guard was called out to prevent African Americans from entering the school. **4.** President Dwight D. Eisenhower ordered the army into Little Rock to enforce the court order, and African American children finally **entered** the school with the protection of federal troops. **5.** State-supported resistance to desegregation **did** not **end** with the Little Rock case. **6.** However, over the years the courts **have** consistently **ruled** in favor of desegregation. **7.** Racial integration of schools **remains** a concern for the current generation as well. **8.** Recent statistics **show** that about 35 percent of African American students go to schools in which 90 percent of the student body is nonwhite. **9.** In addition, support for integration **is declining** OR **has declined** in the current political climate. **10.** Today, the fight for desegregation **has been** largely **replaced** by the fight for quality education for all students.

EXERCISE 6.22 Participles

1. signaling **2.** cheering **3.** catching **4.** parading **5.** Smiling **6.** Carrying **7.** waving **8.** featuring **9.** marching **10.** rumbling

EXERCISE 6.23 Participles

1. Carrying **2.** growling **3.** noticing **4.** overflowing **5.** Wandering **6.** eating **7.** roaming **8.** picnicking **9.** looking **10.** finishing

EXERCISE 6.24 Participial Adjectives

1. excited **2.** soothing **3.** terrified **4.** tired **5.** observing **6.** shaking **7.** amazing **8.** horrifying **9.** satisfying **10.** surprised

EXERCISE 6.25 Participial Adjectives

1. Suffering patients have been used for medical students' practice in teaching hospitals for decades. **2.** Correct **3.** Sitting in a **packed** lecture hall, first- and second-year medical students can only imagine working on a real patient. **4.** However, **disgusted** patients soon tire of having amateurs use them to practice starting IVs, drawing blood, and giving injections. **5.** Correct **6.** Correct **7.** A **distressed** medical student may choke a mechanical patient repeatedly while trying to put a tube down its throat, and the machine will utter a loud gagging noise. **8.** The gagging sound is **unnerving**, but students' mistakes do not hurt any living human beings. **9.** The **uncomplaining** mechanical patients allow students to develop good medical techniques before they handle real people. **10.** When these teaching techniques become more widespread, hospitalized people all over the United States will be **relieved**.

EXERCISE 6.26 Infinitives and Gerunds

Since a university education in one country may differ from a university experience in another, students studying outside their native country may struggle **to understand** educational attitudes within foreign institutions. For example, in some countries students are expected **to avoid speaking** in class, but in other countries it is expected, if not required. Moreover, instructors in some countries encourage students **to participate** actively by **solving** problems in groups, **making** presentations, and **examining** case studies.

Another aspect of the foreign classroom that is often confusing is the teacher-student relationship. In many countries this relationship is a formal one; in other countries it can appear **to be** more relaxed. Regardless of the level of formality between teacher and student, students should remember **to meet** deadlines for assignments and **to treat** the professor with respect. Even if a professor meets with students outside of class **to have** coffee with them, this shouldn't make the professor appear **to be** any less of an authority figure.

EXERCISE 6.27 Infinitives and Gerunds

1. to work **2.** to share **3.** to collaborate **4.** plagiarizing **5.** cheating **6.** to do **7.** to judge **8.** working **9.** asking **10.** angering

EXERCISE 6.28 Infinitives and Gerunds

1. International students who are considering **studying** in the United States should realize that relationships between students here can be either cooperative or competitive, depending on the class. **2.** International students who expect **to cooperate** with classmates may initially feel uncomfortable with the competition in American schools. **3.** Of course, they should not hesitate **to ask** their classmates for help. **4.** In some courses, however, the instructor might decide **to calculate** students' grades in relation to one another. **5.** This method of **grading** is called a "curve." **6.** When a curve is used, students may be reluctant **to share** their lecture notes with others because they don't want to hurt their own grades. **7.** Students without high grade-point averages risk not **getting** into a top graduate program. **8.** Employers trying to fill a job opening may also choose **to look** at a candidate's grade-point average and faculty recommendations. **9.** When students under pressure are asked **to decide** between helping classmates and decreasing competition for a high grade-point average, they often choose the latter. **10.** International students sometimes have to get used to **functioning** in this competitive system.

Part 7 Modifiers

EXERCISE 7.1 Determiners

Historically, Japan has not been **a** country that encouraged immigration. **The** current labor shortage, however, may force **that** country to start allowing immigration. Because of **Japan's** low birthrate, not enough new workers are entering **the** workforce. Then, when women do have children, **few** new mothers stay in **the** job market. In addition, **Japan's** population is aging faster than **the** population of any other developed nation. Soon, **four** times as many Japanese citizens will be over age sixty-five as will be under **that** age. For **these three** reasons, **the** country will not be able to achieve economic growth or support itself unless it expands **its** labor pool. What strategy would have **a** more immediate effect than inviting immigration?

EXERCISE 7.2 Determiners

1. children's 2. a 3. many 4. X 5. a 6. their 7. Many 8. a 9. All 10. this; America's

EXERCISE 7.3 Determiners

1. **Many** businesses today expect executives to be good public speakers. 2. In fact, **a** person who cannot speak well in public is unlikely to be promoted to an executive position. 3. However, 40 percent of all Americans have **a** terrible fear of public speaking. 4. For these people, giving **a** speech is usually a miserable experience. 5. Experts suggest a **few** ways to help conquer a fear of public speaking. 6. Taking **a** few deep breaths before a speech gives the speaker extra oxygen and can calm nerves. 7. Some speakers feel more confident when they imagine the audience in **their** underwear. 8. When speakers remember something that made them laugh recently, **the** funny memory can help them to relax. 9. People who have [**no determiner necessary**] extreme problems with public speaking might need professional help. 10. Many organizations can help to conquer a **businessperson's** fear of giving speeches.

EXERCISE 7.4 Determiners

1. a few 2. a little 3. any 4. a few 5. a little 6. any 7. any 8. a few 9. any 10. a little

EXERCISE 7.5 Determiners

1. a few 2. a few 3. a little 4. any 5. A little 6. any 7. a few 8. any 9. a few 10. any

EXERCISE 7.6 Determiners

1. Many 2. many 3. much 4. Some 5. many 6. Some 7. many 8. much 9. many 10. much

EXERCISE 7.7 Determiners

1. some 2. any 3. some 4. any 5. some 6. some 7. Some 8. any 9. any 10. some

EXERCISE 7.8 Determiners

1. this 2. those 3. this 4. this 5. these 6. this 7. that 8. that 9. these 10. this

EXERCISE 7.9 Determiners

1. this 2. these 3. those 4. this 5. that 6. these 7. those 8. that 9. that 10. this

EXERCISE 7.10 Determiners

1. This 2. these 3. this 4. This 5. these 6. These 7. this 8. this 9. these 10. This

EXERCISE 7.11 Adjectives

1. tattered jersey 2. faded number 3. school mascot 4. all students 5. basketball game 6. final game 7. shortest member 8. star player 9. unbelievable shot 10. terrific game

EXERCISE 7.12 Adjectives

1. overstuffed backpack 2. fashion magazine 3. research paper 4. dirty look 5. rough draft 6. unruly mess; old sandwich 7. crumpled draft 8. two days 9. best work 10. next time

EXERCISE 7.13 Adjectives

Possible Answers 1. Most people with attention deficit disorder display **obvious** behavioral symptoms such as hyperactivity, disorganization, impulsiveness, and an inability to manage time effectively. 2. **All** these symptoms affect performance in certain jobs. 3. A.D.D. was once thought to exist only in a few **troublesome** children, but now experts believe that adults can also suffer from it. 4. Nowadays, new research and openness about the condition help prevent **potential** job discrimination. 5. Most adults would have trouble remaining completely focused on a **boring** thirty-minute slide presentation. **6.** For an adult with A.D.D., such a task is a **huge** cognitive burden. **7. Simple** modifications in the work routine can help A.D.D. sufferers to be more effective in their job. **8.** Organizing paperwork by color and size clears up **some** kinds of confusion for A.D.D. sufferers. **9.** For example, a **large** green folder might contain invoices, and a small blue folder could hold receipts. **10.** If it is not possible for them to change **confusing** daily office routines, A.D.D. sufferers should consider changing careers.

EXERCISE 7.14 Adjectives

The **black** crow called loudly from the shoulder of the **faded** scarecrow. The **neglected** garden had not been tended in years. Vegetables no longer grew in **neat** rows, because weeds and briars had taken their places. In **early** autumn, the house was put up for sale. One day, a car pulled into the driveway, and a **young** couple got out. They immediately loved the house and its garden. "This is perfect!" said the man to his **cheerful** wife, and she agreed. They bought the house and began to tend the **vegetable** garden at once. By summertime, the house was once again lovely, and vegetables were again growing in the **beautiful** garden.

EXERCISE 7.15 Adjectives

The origin of the roller coaster is an **interesting** one. **Early** roller coasters, in fact, did not roll at all. They were slides made from **hard** wood and then covered with **layered** sheets of ice. **Brave** riders would climb stairs leading up to the back of the slides. Once at the top, the passengers would rocket down the **frightening** 50-degree drop and then climb an **additional** set of stairs leading to the **next** slide. These **thrilling** slides were a favorite of Catherine the Great, and legend has it that she had **several** slides constructed on her estate to entertain guests.

EXERCISE 7.16 Adverbs

1. slowly turned **2.** eerily creaked **3.** loudly called **4.** finally answered **5.** briskly walking **6.** regularly spent **7.** affectionately known **8.** thoroughly enjoyed **9.** suddenly died **10.** especially enjoyed

EXERCISE 7.17 Adverbs

1. quickly put **2.** patiently waiting **3.** proudly said **4.** speedily made **5.** promptly met **6.** excitedly asked **7.** knowingly patted **8.** brightly led **9.** recently discovered **10.** wildly applauded

EXERCISE 7.18 Adverbs

Gus University is **extremely** proud of its men's track team, **especially** the star of the team, Andre. Andre runs very **fast**. In fact, he **recently** set a new record at Gus U for the 50-yard dash. **Today**, he is competing in the state meet. **Supposedly**, Olympic scouts are coming to watch him run. Coach Vasquez will be looking around **nervously**, trying to detect the scouts. **Fortunately**, Andre is more focused than his coach. **Calmly**, he will stretch his legs, arms, and body in preparation for his main event, the 50-yard dash. If Andre wins, he will **graciously** accept the handshakes of Coach Vasquez and me, the incognito Olympic scout.

EXERCISE 7.19 Adverbs

Traditionally, in this school district, Field Day is a competition among local high schools. Every year, students **eagerly** await it. Our coaches talk about team spirit and sportsmanship, but even so the events are **fiercely** competitive. They include track and field events as well as a tug of war. The events move **quickly**. Competitors **anxiously** wait for their scores. Murray High School has **consistently** won Field Day, so of course everyone wants to beat them. But this year might be their year to lose. A new event has **recently** been added: a poster contest. It means that even nonathletic students can **actively** participate in Field Day. The winning poster will be awarded 100 points. Who knows, maybe this year Murray High School can be stopped.

Part 8 Prepositions

EXERCISE 8.1 Prepositions

1. X 2. of 3. with 4. with 5. in 6. in 7. from; to 8. to 9. in 10. about

EXERCISE 8.2 Prepositions

1. Some parents don't make any effort to understand [**no preposition necessary**] teenagers. 2. **In** such situations, the workplace can provide a place for teens to interact with adult role models. 3. At work, teenagers can learn to form relationships **with** other people. 4. While they are in high school, students spend a lot of time **with** their friends or in class. 5. Work, **on** the other hand, often requires teenagers to cooperate with people they may not know or like very well. 6. Working also gives students something to do **in** (OR **during**) the hours after school. 7. Teenagers with nothing to do after school are more likely to get **in** (OR **into**) trouble. 8. A part-time job can allow teens to pay **for** leisure activities that they would otherwise be unable to afford. 9. Having a little money to spend **on** things they want or need makes teenagers feel more independent. 10. A teenager's ability to succeed both as a student and as a worker depends largely **on** his or her sense of responsibility.

EXERCISE 8.3 Prepositions

Frank Stoeber is responsible **for** one of the greatest roadside attractions **in** the state of Kansas. A farmer **by** trade, Frank would save pieces of string by rolling them **into** a ball. The more string that Frank would add, the larger the ball would grow. Instead of using the ball of string **for** other projects, Frank continued to add **to** it. When Frank donated the ball of string to the town **of** Cawker City, it was enormous. **Over** one and a half million feet of string was rolled **within** a ball that was eleven feet wide. It was the largest ball of string in Kansas. To ward **off** any potential record breakers, Cawker City holds an annual Twine-A-Thon so that the famous ball of string started by Frank Stoeber can continue to grow.

EXERCISE 8.4 Prepositions

1. for 2. about 3. of 4. to 5. to 6. on; on 7. in 8. in 9. of 10. about

EXERCISE 8.5 Idiomatic Verbs

1. up 2. off 3. out 4. to 5. up 6. with 7. into 8. up with 9. out 10. down

EXERCISE 8.6 Idiomatic Verbs

1. out 2. up 3. into 4. on 5. out 6. out 7. up 8. down 9. over 10. out

EXERCISE 8.7 Idiomatic Verbs

1. My idea was that kids who smoked cigarettes turned **out** to be the coolest kids in school. 2. They came **out** with unusual things to say and they wore cool clothes. 3. I admired them so much that I would go **along** with whatever they said we should think or do. 4. One day I put **on** my coolest clothes and decided to try a cigarette, too. 5. I looked **forward** to being more like them. 6. But when I tried it, the cigarette tasted so disgusting that I wanted to throw up. 7. I started to look at those kids in a new way, and I no longer wanted to take **after** them. 8. They did not seem to notice that I did not want to hang **out** OR **around** with them anymore. 9. I realized that I had put **up** with their silly ideas for a long time. 10. From that day on, I decided to stick **with** friends who did not try so hard to be cool.